SONS OF THE FLAG

by

RYAN
"BIRDMAN"
PARROTT

SONS OF THE FLAG

by

RYAN "BIRDMAN" PARROTT

Preslyn Publishing

Cover art by Desiree Byrd

Cover photo by permission from Dan Pope

Editing and layout by Jonathan Peters, PhD
        www.JonathanPetersPhD.com

Proofed by Lulu from The Proofreaders, LLC, and Patrick Parrott

ISBN: 978-0983789314
Printed in the United States of America

Dedication

This book is dedicated to the ones who mean the most to me:

To my mother, Lisa, and my father, Patrick. You raised me to never give up, and in turn, you never gave up on me.

To Robert Raymond. You proved to me that outside the service, a friendship can be as strong as one inside.

To Vic Lattimore. Words can't describe how much you've done for me and my family. But I'm still a better shooter than you.

To Steve Woods, as Chairman of Sons of the Flag's organization, you have given me the room to grow and lead our organization and have made every promise a reality.

To Ace and the Lane boys. Coolest men on the mountain!

To Pryor Blackwell. You're one of my closest brothers. "ROGER THAT."

To Vlada. With you, my life is fulfilled.

To our soldiers and first responders. Thank you for your devotion and undying sacrifice to our nation. Without you, America would not be a glorious nation.

In memory of Buckaroo and Dutch, my two grandfathers

TABLE OF CONTENTS

FOREWORD

"It isn't the reward that matters or the recognition you might harvest. It is your depth of commitment, your quality of service, the product of your devotion—these are the things that count in life. When you give purely, the honor comes in the giving, and that is honor enough."
— Scott O'Grady, retired Air Force captain

Throughout history, whenever this nation has needed great people to step up, great people didn't disappoint. Possessing a unique brand of American courage, these men and women found themselves able to accomplish feats few would dare to even consider. They held their principles far above their hope for popularity. For some, virtue drove them to actions that placed their very lives at risk. These actions came not from a desire for medals, glory, or fame, but to answer the questions: "If not me, who? If not here, where? If not now, when?"

American courage has many faces—political, social, physical, intellectual, and most importantly, moral—but it unfailingly stems from a deep sense of humility, service, and sacrifice, as well as the drive to give back to God and to this great American society. It seeks to pay one's debt for living in such a blessed and bountiful land.

Now as never before, American society needs great role models. Now as never before, we need great Americans like those you'll find in this amazing book. The heroes in this book answered the above "if" questions as children. Now as adults, they live those virtues.

Today the spiritual descendants of the Founding Fathers and the Sons of Liberty passionately seek to defend our great nation. Some find themselves enlisting in our military. Others look to defend our nation through the public safety sectors of police, EMS, and firefighting. They willingly give of their time, their talent, and when necessary, their lives.

> "You will never do anything in this world without courage. It is the greatest quality of the mind next to honor."
>
> —Aristotle

With the greatest respect and humility I would like to share an amazing, inspiring, and heroic story similar to those shared in this book.

As the dust settled on September 11, 2001, weary firefighters, stunned and confused, were searching through the rubble for any sign of survivors. Among those searching was a former NYPD police officer, now an FDNY firefighter, Chris Engledrum. Chris had also served in the US Army and was deployed in 1990 as a paratrooper with the 82nd Airborne.

On that tragic day in September, alongside his fellow surviving firefighters from Ladder 61, Chris searched through the debris for his fallen brothers. When another firefighter came across an American flag in the rubble, Chris called Captain Mike Dugan and asked where they could raise this flag. Captain Dugan grabbed a nearby ladder and threw it up on one of the few light posts still standing in the wreckage.

> "The nation today needs men who think in terms of service to their country and not in terms of their country's debt to them."
> —General Omar Bradley

With Chris bucking the ladder, they raised that flag.

This is not the flag from the iconic photo you all have seen, but a precursor to it. This was a flag raised just moments after the collapse of the towers, while the dust was still heavy in the air, while the wounded were still looking for treatment and the survivors were still struggling to rescue anyone they could. This was the first flag raised over Ground Zero in defiance of those who would try to hurt us. It was raised—instinctively, loyally, courageously—by men of character.

Several weeks later, Chris would learn that members of his old Army unit were going to fill the legendary 69th New York Irish Brigade for duty in Iraq. Chris couldn't let his old teammates go without him, so he reenlisted with the Fighting 69th.

On November 29, 2004, the armored Humvee® carrying Chris and two other firefighters (fellow firefighters Specialist Wilfredo Urbina and Daniel Swift of Ladder 43) as well as three other soldiers was hit by an improvised explosive device. Chris and Wilfredo were killed. Chris was on that mission because he could not let his comrades fight without him. He had been compelled by a sense of loyalty, of duty, of honor, of being called to service. This is the same moral imperative shared by all those who serve and by the men in this book.

As you continue through this amazing book, it will become glaringly apparent that none of these American heroes were driven by expectations of recognition and reward; instead, what drove them was a sense of duty and a sense of loyalty to their respective communities and to one another. What motivated them will continue to garner the respect and admiration of American generations for centuries to come.

In every city, town, village, and county, Americans continue to perform acts of ordinary and extraordinary courage, loyalty, duty, selflessness, and honor. As we ready ourselves to read the pages that follow, we should remember that thousands of flags have been folded solemnly and handed to grieving families.

God bless all those who serve, and may He continue to bless these United States of America, the greatest nation in the history of the world, not for her power but for her love, justice, and service to liberty and humanity.

—*Chief Bobby Halton*
Editor-in-Chief of *Fire Engineering* magazine

INTRODUCTION

The difference between American soldiers and the enemy is that enemy soldiers/terrorists might believe in their so-called mission, but they certainly don't believe in each other.

I served eight years as a US Navy SEAL. People love to ask me about that time. I get bombarded with requests for details about the missions, the enemy, the firefights, and yes, the killings. Over and over, different people ask the same questions about what I did over there. What no one ever asks me is why I did it.

It's an intriguing question. If you think about it, why would anyone join the military with such a strong risk of being severely wounded or killed? And why, in the heat of battle with your life on the line, would anyone bother to see the mission through?

What is the *why* behind service? It seems important, but the question goes unasked. Maybe, in a time when we seem less like a *United* States, but more like red states versus blue states, in a time where people fight only for their own interests, in a time when we have television shows dedicated to people selfishly ignoring the plight of their fellow citizens, it doesn't cross the mind of the average American to ask soldiers why they volunteer to fight for their country.

> "American soldiers in battle don't fight for what some president says on TV, they don't fight for mom, apple pie, the American flag...they fight for one another."
>
> —LTC Hal Moore

Still, I wonder how I would answer if anyone ever asked me. And how would other veterans answer? How do you describe wanting to support your country, your mission, your brothers-in-arms?

When I found myself having the opportunity to speak with men from each of America's wars in the last 80 years (including two first responders to the biggest attack on American soil: 9/11), I decided to ask the question. How they answered and how their answers compare with my own are the inspiration for this book.

In this book, you will hear the stories of some amazing men who received the call and courageously pursued their mission. These are humble men, reluctant to tell about their heroics, but passionate to share a message about why they served, what their country means to them, and the importance of brotherhood. Their stories inspire me. I'm honored not only to have worked with these men, but also to count them as brothers.

Each chapter tells an individual's story in his own words. I provide introductions to give you a flavor of their personalities; following each story, I share similar experiences from my own story. It is impossible to share the *why* behind our stories without also sharing some of the *what*—the enemies fought, the heroics performed, the medals earned. But as you read these pages, keep in mind the goal behind our telling.

The men in this book want to share the meaning of their service. They hope that their stories will inspire you, not entertain you. So if you're looking for detailed stories about how we took down the enemy, you won't find them here. For my part, I will share how the military trained me to serve the men on my right and left. Unlike other books by Navy SEALs, I won't be sharing how we kicked in doors and brought down bad people. Those stories are being told by others.

Instead, my mission with this book is to bring back to America what I believe it has lost: responsibility for our fellow citizens. The military defines brotherhood as taking responsibility for the person on your left and on your right, making sure they come home safe. Imagine if Americans took that kind of responsibility. Instead of thinking about themselves, what they "deserve," what if they watched out for the people on their left and right? Communities would be stronger. We would watch out for one another. There would be pride in our country again.

With this book, I hope to show how the military and other organizations like police and firefighters have kept alive that which makes this country great: the importance of mission and the values of patriotism and brotherhood.

I want to illustrate the single chain of commitment and dedication that has passed from generation to generation. Military tactics may have changed, the equipment has improved, the enemy is certainly different, but the soldier's dedication remains the same. Finally, I hope to share with America the *why* of service: Why young people volunteer to fight for their country, why firemen selflessly rush to save others, and most importantly, why America as a whole should return to the values of patriotism and brotherhood.

But to begin, I need to share how I first came in contact with the heroic men in these pages. It all began with a recurring daydream:

Across the expanse of the November sky, a plane engine roars. The wind rushes. One by one, a gathering of veterans, each from a different US war, leaps. In the air they are all connected, jump line to jump line. In that moment right before their chutes are pulled, they free-fall together, silhouetted against the bright blue sky above our great nation.

CHAPTER 1

A VISION BORN

I'm told it's called a "Daisy Chain." A former Green Beret, Tony Bandiera, recounting a story from the Vietnam War, explained it to me. It's a skydive maneuver where, instead of locking into the plane, you hook your line to the buddy behind you. The only person who is hooked to the plane is the rear jumper. This means everyone leaps out of the plane tied to the guy behind him. Everyone free-falls until the last guy leaps. As his chute gets pulled, the drag from his chute pulls the chute of the guy in front of him. The chutes pull down the line until the first guy's chute is pulled.

It is an extremely dangerous maneuver, and I've never seen it done.

"We should do it one of these days," Tony insisted. This crazy Vietnam vet still wants to do stuff like that—it's why I love him.

"I'm in," I told him. "I don't know how we are going to do it. But I'm in."

I thought about it a lot. I loved skydiving as a SEAL. In the job I took after leaving the service where I trained law enforcement and civilians in self-defense tactics, I would lean back in my chair and daydream about the daisy-chain jump. I thought it would be fun to get some military veterans together to do a jump like that.

> "Leadership is the art of getting someone else to do something you want done because he wants to do it."
>
> —Dwight Eisenhower

One day, months after first envisioning the veterans jump, I was looking at an iconic picture of a static line jump. The picture showed these men ready to take action in support of one another. Looking at it, I thought, "Man, there should be guys from each of the wars in the picture, jumping together to represent the last 100 years of protecting the nation."

That was when the idea was born: I could coordinate a jump with veterans representing the wars of US history. And I could do it on Veterans Day in honor of our military!

Once I had this idea, it wouldn't leave me alone. But how could I pull it off?

As I continued to think about it, I remembered an amazing man named John Walters III. He was a New York firefighter from Rescue 1 who'd worked through the rubble of 9/11. I thought, "If we are going to put a soldier from every war in this mix, a fireman from 9/11 should be there." It was firemen who'd stepped up when the enemy came to us. They worked tirelessly to restore order and confidence to Americans. So I added firemen to the list of veterans we'd honor.

The vision of this jump was the easy part; the reality was something completely different. How in the heck could I get jumpers from every war, especially in the wars where I didn't know anyone, like Desert Storm, Korea, and World War II?

As I began to work out the logistics in my head, other problems became clear. Even if I could find a willing veteran from each war, what if he hadn't jumped out of a plane before? That would mean we couldn't do it as a static line jump, but would have to do tandem jumps with professional jumpers. It all seemed too much to accomplish. I just didn't have the time or the resources to make this dream a reality. I had to put the idea on hold.

And yet, it wouldn't leave me alone.

When I became president/CEO of Sons of the Flag, an organization dedicated to aiding burn survivors, I found we needed an event to draw attention to our mission. I remembered my idea. I told my team, "We're going to do this. This is our event. It's never been done, and we are going to be the ones to do it."

Now that I was motivated and had a team to support me, I started calling everyone I could think of to put a jump team together. I needed a veteran from each war who would be, as the saying goes, stupid enough to jump out of a perfectly good airplane.

As you can imagine, I ran into a lot of resistance. And the footwork reaching people from some of the older wars was tough. But something incredible was happening along the way; not only was I receiving a lot of support and encouragement and coming in contact with wonderful people, but also I was hearing amazing stories. It was unbelievably empowering hearing these soldiers' stories, even those who couldn't do the jump because of injuries or medical complications or age.

My daydream was becoming a reality. I was getting our team together for what we were calling the "Legacy Jump." But another dream was brewing: sharing the inspirational stories of the men who joined the team. In the chapters that follow, you will learn the reasons why they answered the call and why I felt it was important enough to draw attention to these heroes on Veterans Day.

As a veteran, no matter how old you are, whether you served in conflict, or what walk of life you come from, we all come together to support our brothers. These are the stories of just some of the Sons of the Flag. I hope that you're as inspired by their stories as I was while working with these amazing soldiers.

CHAPTER 2

ANSWERING THE CALL

People who serve their country have their own motivations and their own stories. In the coming chapters, you will hear how some iconic men came to serve. Each story will be an inspiration.

I didn't originally have the desire to serve. While I had great respect for my grandfathers, who both served in World War II, I didn't have a desire to be a soldier when I was growing up.

In fact, I was pretty much a screw-up when I was in high school. I had no vision of where I was headed and no dedication to myself, my community, my country, or God. I was just about having a good time.

One man turned all of that around for me. Because of his love for his country and his desire to inspire his students to do better, he was able to get through to me and change the direction of my life.

I was failing most of my classes in high school. It wasn't that I was a bad person; I would just rather drink alcohol and goof off than go to school. My parents and teachers tried to get through to me, but school wasn't my thing. I remember my dad sitting down with me before a test. Whatever he taught me, I would get. It was the only way I could keep from flunking out of school.

One report card had 15 Fs by the end of the fourth quarter. I was literally that bad. My dad kept my report

Report Card

CHIPPEWA VALLEY HIGH SCHOOL
PARROTT, RYAN C.
STU# 3444   GRADE 11

FOURTH MARKI
FROM 04/02/0

Pd / Class	Teacher	1ST QTR	2ND QTR	1ST EXM	1ST SEM	3RD QTR	4TH QTR	2ND EXM	2ND SEM
1.MARKETING I		C	F	F	F				
1.INTEGR MATH 1B						F	NC		WF
1.STUDY HALL 1B									NC
2.INTEGR MATH 1A		C+	C	D	C				
2.COMPUTER APPLIC						B	F	B	C-
3.MOTIV PSYCH		B	C	B+	B				
3.SPEECH						D	D	D-	D
4.CIVIL WAR		F	C+	A	C-				
4.HEALTH						A	A	B+	A
5.SHAKESPEARE		C-	C+	C	C				
5.ENGLISH 10B						F	F	F	F
6.ENGLISH 10A		F	F	F	F				
6.CREAT WRITING						B	F	C	D

FOURTH QUARTER GPA - 1.00

Eight straight Fs in English, and then I write a book. Go figure.

cards knowing someday I would succeed and he'd remind me how far I'd come.

Everything changed for me when I took Tom Barnes's class my junior year of high school. The class was motivational psychology. It was designed to prepare students for hardship later in life. We learned how to set higher personal standards and develop good work ethics.

Mr. Barnes had been a Marine back in Vietnam. He loved his country. There were American flags all over the classroom. During class he'd get excited about his country, grab a flag, and run around the room telling us how much he loved his country, the Marines, and how satisfying it was to be part of a brotherhood. He was that kind of guy: motivated and inspirational.

I've never seen any other teacher work as hard as Mr. Barnes. He would show up at school way before the students got there and using the entire whiteboard surface, write small cursive letters from top to bottom with the notes that we could take and use to study. I respected Mr. Barnes and listened to his life instructions and his stories, but that was as far as it went for me.

One specific day, I believe Mr. Barnes was focused on me. He picked up the American flag like he usually did, but on this day he didn't run around. He just walked up to the front of the room and held the flag for everyone to see. He looked at each one of us and said, "Ladies and gentlemen, there's only one thing better than the US Marine Corps, and that's becoming a Navy SEAL."

I was like, "What? Did he just say there was something better than his beloved Marine Corps?"

He went on to tell us how the SEALs did crazy stuff that separates them from other soldiers—how they can hold their breaths underwater for unbelievable amounts of time, survive extreme cold, stuff like that.

I thought, "I'm that guy; that's me. I may not be a scholar, but I could totally do the cool stuff that SEALs do."

I was so excited that at the end of class I went up to his desk and said, "Mr. Barnes, I want to be a SEAL."

He said, "Ah, I don't know, man; they're pretty tough."

And I said, "No, dude; I can totally do it. I've got it."

"That's great, Ryan, but that's not something you just walk into. You have to be selected to go into that line of service. If you really want to look into it, I will get you a book on the SEALs."

I wasn't defeated by what he was saying. If anything, I took it as a challenge. I wanted him to believe that I could do it. Maybe that was me being immature or maybe I subconsciously desired to become part of something great. I do know that at that moment, on that day, I began my journey toward becoming part of a brotherhood.

Fortunately, Mr. Barnes remembered our conversation. At the beginning of school a couple days later, there was a copy of *Reader's Digest* on my desk with an article about making it through the toughest training ever. I read the article and was fired up. I knew that this was exactly what I wanted to do.

I showed my dad the article, and he said, "Well, that sounds pretty tough. With such a high attrition rate, maybe you should check out the Marine Corps. You've really never shown a track record for excellence." It was his way of challenging me to get my act together.

The problem was, he was right. While I was fired up that week to become a SEAL, in a short time I was back to screwing off and failing.

I remember I was out partying one night, drunk off my ass. One of my buddies, Jeff Malczynski (we called him "Corn Nuts"), sat down next to me and asked, "You drunk?"

I said, "Yeah."

He looked at me and said, "How the hell are you ever going to become a Navy SEAL while you're doing this dumb shit?" Then he got up and left.

That hurt. But he got through. And I listened.

I went home and slept it off. The next morning I went to church with my mom and then I got myself a membership at the YMCA. From that day on, I trained every single day as hard as I could. My teachers had all gotten together to get me on a plan to get my grades back up, and I started

Before graduation, I visited John F. Kennedy's eternal flame because he is the president who established the Navy SEALs.

working through their plan.

And then came September 11, 2001. I was sitting in typing class when the TV in the room showed a building burning in flames. Our class watched as a plane came crashing into a second tower, exploding in flames. The media alerted us that the planes were a possible terrorist attack.

When I heard that, I got up and took off down the hall. My government teacher grabbed me as I passed and asked, "Mr. Parrott, where the hell do you think you're going?"

I said, "Did you see what happened to our country today? I'm going to enlist in the United States Navy."

He let go of my arm, and I ran out the doors as fast as I could.

I drove straight to the recruiter's office. When I burst in, the recruiter knew exactly why I was there. We sat down and started getting the paperwork together.

Though I didn't sign up that day, that was the day that I committed to being part of the brotherhood. I knew that I would have to get consent from my parents and that I still had to finish high school, but I was committed. Months of hard work lay in front of me, but I had a direc-

My best buddy, Jake, on the left, passed away when I was in SEAL training. It was my first taste of losing a brother.

tion and I was motivated.

I went on to graduate from high school on the honor roll. I am extremely grateful for my teachers' support, and I owe Mr. Barnes more than words can describe. Corn Nuts, you are my hero.

On September 4, 2002, I enlisted in the Navy. My family on both sides were there to see me get sworn in. The thing that really touched me was that both of my grandfathers were also there.

While I was filling out the rest of my papers that day, my family went out to get some food. Before they returned, I was loaded on a bus and driven to the airport with a one-way ticket to Great Lakes, Illinois, to begin Basic Training. I didn't even get to say goodbye. That was tough, but I had a goal, and I was that much closer to being a SEAL.

This picture was taken moments before my family left to get some food. It was the last time I saw them before being shipped out.

CHAPTER 3

SALVATORE GIUNTA
Afghanistan

INTRODUCTION:

You are lucky if you meet a hero in your lifetime. You will memorize their stories and share their message with others. When you are having a bad day, you will gain inspiration from their experiences.

I'm not only honored to be sharing the stories of the different men in this book, I consider each of them a friend. I'm humbled by their acceptance of me.

Our first soldier is Salvatore Giunta. I'm extremely lucky to be able to call this true American hero my friend. He is the first living recipient of the Medal of Honor since the Vietnam War. From that war to Sal's award, the nine other Medals of Honor were given posthumously.

As soldiers, we don't do it for the medals. We're almost embarrassed by our medals. Yes, they are an honor, but we get them at a cost. And that is certainly true in Sal's case.

While I understand where Sal is coming from when he speaks about how he only received this award with his team standing behind him and his belief that he did nothing more than what his team would have done for him, I also respect what he did for his brothers and his country. Without concern for himself, he rushed into a wall of bullets to save a member of his team.

I met Sal at a Medal of Honor dinner. I was honored just to be there with him and even more honored when I got the opportunity to shake his hand. I can't express how blown away I was when he flew to Dallas to jump in the Legacy Jump and by his willingness to be included in this book representing the Afghan War.

To get a feel for what kind of a man Sal is, I encourage you to look up his book, *Living with Honor*. You'll learn about his motivation and dedication, his humbleness, and the burden he carries for his fallen friends and teammates. Then you'll understand how inspired I am by this man and honored that he has shared his story in these pages.

AFGHANISTAN:

Unlike some of the other guys in this book, I grew up in a family who had no history of military service. The military was just something I saw on TV and it didn't necessarily appeal to me.

When 9/11 happened, I was a junior in high school. I remember sitting in chemistry class and being told that a plane flew into a building. I think everyone thought it was a terrible accident at first. We turned on the TV, and it wasn't just a small plane crashing into a building; it was a huge plane and a huge building.

As we watched, the second plane came in and hit the second tower, and I had the immediate sense that this was not an accident—this was not a mistake. This was blatant disregard for America and our people. It was an attack.

I got fired up. I wanted everything to be different. I had the feeling that I needed to get out there and do something. This was my chance to make a difference. This was my generation's Pearl Harbor, and someone should answer the call.

I was 16 at the time, turning 17 in January. I was too young to join the military. I needed to graduate from high school, to worry about the test next week, to worry about my girlfriend, and to do what my parents said.

The following year in high school, my senior year, I was working at a Subway restaurant. It was 9:30 or 10 at night and this radio commercial came on saying something like, "Come on down and see your Army recruiter and get a free T-shirt."

I thought, "I should go and do that. Who doesn't want a free T-shirt?"

I went into the recruiting station the next day, and the recruiter told me, "We are a country at war. You are an able-bodied male. If you want to make a difference, this is it. You can make a tangible difference right off the bat."

I was like, "Well, I'm not going to work at Subway for life, but I don't know if this is such a good idea. Still, it couldn't hurt to take the test."

I got the scores about 10 days later. I went back to the recruiter, and he broke down the numbers. He said, "Hey, man, you got a 124 GT score. You can do whatever you want in the military."

We talked a little bit longer. I thought, "I can make a decision right here, today, to make a difference."

I didn't know anything about the military, so I didn't know fully what I was getting into. When they asked me what I wanted to do, I looked up and saw the parachute on the ceiling of the recruiting office. I decided I wanted to jump out of planes, shoot guns, sleep on the dirt, that kind of stuff.

He said, "That's airborne infantry."

So I signed my papers and did all the physical stuff within the week. I was committed.

Yes, I was young and naïve. I was excited to go to war, to take care of business and then come home, drink beer, and chase a pretty girl. My motivation was the opportunity to do something for my country, to put my life into something fully.

When I initially joined the airborne infantry, I didn't care where they sent me. I didn't realize that just because

I did five jumps in jump school, they wouldn't necessarily send me to war.

Next, I was sent to Italy with the 173rd Airborne Infantry Brigade. When I arrived in May of 2004, I was surrounded by thousands of men who had had combat experience in Iraq; meanwhile, I was just doing a lot of push-ups and listening to their stories. I learned a lot of valuable lessons from them and gained a stronger sense of responsibility to my fellow man.

In basic training, you have a battle buddy that you are connected to and you are responsible for, and they're responsible for you. When I first arrived at my unit, I found that that bond has to be unbreakable. I was responsible for the man to the left and the man to the right, and they are responsible for me.

That was the first time in my life when I wasn't caring about just me. I was working with a team—the guys to the left and the right.

Training created bonds of commitment to one another knowing that we will always have each other's back. As long as we are together, no matter how bad it gets, things will eventually be okay. From sports, I knew what it was like to win or lose as a team, but I didn't fully know what it was like to be committed 100 percent to a team.

I went on my first deployment to Afghanistan in the spring of 2005. We were stationed at a place called Baylough, which is just a little mud hut that we took over from the Afghanis. It is 45 to 50 kilometers away from any other American base.

We strung up three lines of wire and called that the perimeter. Then we put up another line inside that one in hopes that the enemy wouldn't just drive over it. We didn't have any electricity or running water. We were just 35 guys in a mud hut in the middle of Afghanistan.

Most of our missions involved formations and walking in the mountains, waiting for them to shoot at us so we could identify who the enemy was. Throughout the first couple of months, we mostly did small arms contact, RPGs, maybe a few indirect assaults, but nothing really close. The majority of contacts were from 300 meters out or more, so it wasn't too terrible.

August 21, 2005, was the first time I saw a dead American soldier. I'd seen dead people before, but they were usually old people, people who were sick, or someone who had a terrible accident who didn't look both ways before crossing the street. I'd never seen our best get taken out.

Another platoon was coming out to bring us some equipment to create better base defenses. We didn't have any vehicles, so we walked everywhere. The vehicles they were dropping off would really help.

Four or five kilometers out, an IED took out the lead truck. It killed four guys and the gunner lost both of his legs. They called us up, but it took a while to get there on foot.

That was a hard day for me. On that day, I felt my own mortality. Up until that time, I thought we were invincible, that bullets bounced off or at least don't hurt that badly. But all of a sudden, that was no longer true. The IEDs are a serious threat, and they were all around us.

The very next week we were notified that a high-value target was in our sector. Command said they were getting pings from a cell phone in a nearby house. When we got there, the company commander yelled for them to come out. And they did with guns blazing. One of our lieutenants was shot in the head.

A week before I had felt safe; now there were bombs in the ground and my leaders are getting killed. I felt almost helpless. I didn't sign up for this, to walk around the mountains getting shot at.

A team leader talked to me. He said, "Look, dude, this is exactly what it is. It was like this in Iraq, and it will be like this until the war is over. You have the opportunity to do it. Don't be afraid. I promise you no matter what, the sun is going to come up tomorrow, whether you are in it or I am, and we can know that we did everything we could."

I don't know how that changed my thinking, but it put it all in perspective. Throughout the history of America there has been the loss of brothers in combat and terror. Soldiers wrote that check; we just hope it won't get cashed.

When he put it into perspective, he reminded me why I was there. I wanted to do this. Giving it 100 percent was all that mattered.

When winter came, it socked us in with snow. We still didn't have electricity or running water, so we turned to survival mode, concentrating on staying warm and fed. We did our patrols, but walking two kilometers in that weather was rough. We were there to fight, but no one wants to fight in the cold and snow. So it got boring.

I remember thinking how much I would rather be doing anything other than waiting through winter. But we were all there together. We did everything we could today because tomorrow was coming. The more you do today, the more you will be capable of achieving tomorrow.

We came back from that deployment in May 2006. I thought things had been timed right so I wouldn't be deployed again before my four years were up. But I found out that I'd signed a clause about stop loss. It said if they needed me, they could keep me. I was pissed. I was like "Dude, I've got a girlfriend, I've got plans. This is not part of my plan."

My buddy stopped me and said, "I want you to know I'm glad you are coming with us." It wasn't that he was happy I wasn't getting what I wanted; instead, he was happy because we were going to be together. Whatever we were going to do, we were going to do together again.

That speaks about the bond of brothers. It's not about what you want, but about how we can do it best with our friends, buddies, brothers, the ones we trained with, and the ones who have been there before. There's something to be said about when bullets are cracking over your head and you look down the line and all you see are friends willing to do what needs to be done.

My second deployment was going to be 15 months. This time, I was in a leadership position. It changed my outlook on how business got done. I was so proud when I got promoted to sergeant. For the first time, I had authority and it was up to me to lead and guide and mentor.

The second deployment was very different. We were in a valley that was six miles by six miles. There were about 140 people in the valley in four locations. And there was small arms fire every day.

We still didn't have running water or electricity, but

Apache helicopters came through regularly. We also didn't have to go on seven-kilometer walks anymore; instead, we only had three-kilometer walks, and we were pretty much guaranteed to get into a fight along the way.

In late October of 2007, things changed. We'd been out for four days. Our job was to stir stuff up and see if people pulled out guns.

Two days earlier, we'd dropped some bombs on a house and there was collateral damage. We had a meeting with the folks in the village and they declared jihad on us. There was going to be no forgiveness. We knew it was going to get worse before it got better. We had lost the faith of the people we were trying to help.

On October 23, we were at the top of the ridge line. There were maybe 20 of us commanding the high ground, making sure we had a 360-perimeter view.

Our scout team and a gun team with a 240 Bravo were overrun. Two soldiers were killed and several wounded. The enemy also got some of our equipment, including night-vision scopes and ammunition.

The next day, 18 of us set off at about two in the morning. Our job was to pull overwatch for another group of 15 to 20 guys who were going into the village below to talk to the elders to see if we could figure out what happened to the gear. We also wanted to talk the villagers off the ledge from hating us.

We sat on the ridge until it was dark again. We didn't get anything from the villagers, so we decided to come down from the ridge and walk back to base. Our Alpha team walked out first, but they were only two guys because guys had been needed back at base as guards. The terrain dictated that we climb through one section on our hands and knees. The enemy knew this, and that's where they ambushed us.

It was a textbook L-shaped ambush, and we were in the middle of it.

It was intense. The world was exploding in those first five seconds. Automatic rifles were shooting at us from their ambush line. We had no cover, no concealment.

The first thing I did was drop down to the ground to cover my guys. They were my first priority.

When you are ambushed, the books say charge the ambush line. In the first couple of seconds, Casey immediately started returning fire with the M249, which shoots about 900 rounds per minute. It was like a dragon blowing fire.

He knew that by doing this, he set himself up as a target. He also knew that if he drew fire, it would give the rest of us some time to set up our defenses. That is true love for your brothers. Casey showed complete disregard for his own safety for us.

As I looked for our team leader, I saw him get shot in the head. He was probably 10 to 15 yards in front of me. I ran to grab him, to bring him back with us, his body at least. But as I grabbed his backpack and started dragging his body, he stumbled to his feet. The bullet had hit his helmet. It had dropped him, but didn't go through the plating. He was dazed, but he wasn't done.

He immediately started yelling for grenades and to move in progress forward. I threw my grenades and moved. But ultimately the grenades went over the enemy because the proximity was just too close and we didn't have a full idea of where our guys were.

When we got to Spc. Eckrode, he was shot twice in the leg and twice in the chest. The team leader got the M249 up and running so we could put more effective fire back on the enemy. We had more things to do than we had people to do them.

I looked around. I couldn't find Brennan. I knew what he had done; he'd charged the line. So I took off running to find Brennan and make sure that he wasn't doing it all alone. I wanted to fight next to him because we are stronger together.

I pushed forward, maybe 25 to 30 meters, to where the ambush line was. I saw three people—two people carrying one person by the arms and legs. I couldn't understand what I was seeing. I just ran closer.

As I got closer, I realized what I was seeing was two enemies carrying sergeant Brennan. So I did what I was trained to do, destroy the enemies of the US. I opened fire on them, killing one of them. The other one dropped Brennan and ran away.

I was not in a position to give chase. We were behind the enemy ambush line. So I grabbed Brennan and took off running in the direction we had come from. By this time, the enemy was starting to retreat and break contact. As they did, they created enough space between us and them for the Apache helicopters to swoop in and do what they do.

I started working on Brennan. He was still talking, but had been shot seven times. We got him medevaced out, but he later died in surgery.

After the helicopter was out, we still had a two-hour walk back. We divided up the extra guns and reconsolidated the ammunition, food, and water. We were all kind of out of it on that walk back. That was a long night.

As Americans, we are blessed and privileged because we don't fight because we hate our enemy. We fight because we love what's behind us. We love our families. We love one another; therefore, we fight to protect what we already have.

I think in my entire military career of seven and a half years, the best example of true service and care and compassion was Casey standing there with total disregard for his own life because of what he was protecting, which was us.

Our Alpha team was no more after that night, so Bravo team became Alpha, and I walked point. That night really rearranged our squad. But we were still strong because our strengths were with each other.

We were all there together, doing it. We knew that they weren't going to quit because the guy on the left and the guy on the right weren't going to quit. If you quit, you only hurt them. We were 100 percent invested in each other. My responsibility was to my country, my mission, and my brothers. Just knowing that they had the same commitment meant that we could move forward, overcome hardships, and face another day.

Everything I ever did over there was for what I thought was right and for the USA.

BIRDMAN:

No honorable soldier is comfortable receiving medals. We don't do what we do to make a name for ourselves, to build ourselves up, or even to secure our futures.

When you are dedicated to the men on your right and left, you know that any honor that you receive can only come from the support you get from your brothers and sisters.

Contrast this with what you see in politics, business, and society. People gladly grab the limelight, pushing themselves up at the expense of others. They seldom acknowledge the people who have supported them and helped them become what they are.

Politics and entertainment would be different if Americans were focused on protecting the persons on their right and left, and if they were dedicated to a mission and less concerned with themselves. Would all these supposed "stars" exist if they had the values of the military, the values that we used to have in America?

When soldiers do their jobs, they know their mission, and they look out for their team. And they know that no mission ever goes 100 percent perfectly. It's not about simply doing your job, but going beyond the standard and stepping forward in times of distress.

Our achievements come because we followed the code of the military—the code that we used to have as Americans. We know that we did what any soldier would have done in the same situation. We were prepared for difficulties and disasters. We simply followed the values we were taught and the training we received. We did what we were supposed to do. Why should we receive a medal for that?

When Sal woke up that morning, it was another day on the job. The enemy was out there, and he had his orders and mission. When the enemy came on strong, he rose to the occasion. Running to save his brother, he was hit with a bullet. He paused for a moment and then pressed on.

How many people do you know at work or society who would do what he did? Most people would say, "I don't get paid enough for this," or "I don't deserve this," or "THEY messed up."

Sal didn't think this. Things went to hell and he said, "My brother needs me." He was shot and he still moved on. Who does that?

My experience with that moment, where you realize you're injured but your brother is in greater danger, is not as dramatic as Sal's. In fact, many soldiers in Afghanistan and Iraq had similar experiences. But the experience did make me the person I am today.

It actually happened on my first real deployment.

We had just completed a 24-hour mission looking for an enemy weapons cache site. Intel said it was on an island in the middle of the river. We snuck out at night, stayed alert throughout the night, then searched the island all day. And we came up empty.

We were finally heading back to base, tired and drained. But we still had to stay alert because we were heading down the most dangerous road called Route Michigan, ironically, the state I grew up in.

This was back in 2005, and because it was a newer war and we weren't sure what we were getting into, our rules

flames, flying out of the top of the Humvee. It was surreal because it was the fastest thing that has ever happened in my life. You can't even think about it, it's so fast. You can't react.

I remember the Humvee lifting off the ground. And I was out of the top of it.

When it landed again, the front of the vehicle was missing, and dirt flew everywhere. It was all dust and soot and fireballs. This was an up-armored Humvee. Had it been an older model, I would not be writing this today.

> "We sleep safely at night because rough men stand ready to visit violence on those who would harm us."
> —Winston Churchill

When the bomb blew the Humvee upward, it launched me straight out of the turret. The first thing they teach you about being in the turret is to hunker down when things heat up. If there is some shooting going on, *you* are the bull's-eye. You're in the open. So you stay low and keep control of your weapon.

With the crashes going on, I had already lowered myself. This position put me closer to the explosion. And unlike my brothers, I had nothing but space above me. When the fireball came, it launched me through the turret.

When I hit the ground, I somehow landed on my feet. Immediately, I reached for my face. I knew something was wrong, just like when you break a bone or cut yourself. But I couldn't see my face. All I could do was reach up and feel the soot and grime, but knowing something was wrong. Then I felt my skin peel away.

But there was nothing I could do about it then. It would

have to wait until later because so much was going on around me. There was that brief pause before the training kicked in and I moved to action.

In the next half-second, I looked over at the Humvee. The front end was still burning and there were guys already around it, some yelling, some quiet.

I ran up to our driver, who was closest to me. He had been launched straight through the door of the Humvee. That's an inch and a half of steel he had gone through. The impact alone was unbelievable.

From what I could tell, his leg was broken. But I couldn't quite tell because my eyes kept watering because the flash that burned my face also burned my eyes.

I could see there was skin missing and bones were exposed. But I couldn't tell why he was in so much pain until I tore his pants leg open. He was bleeding from what appeared to be his femoral artery.

Our medic came running up on my side, "What've you got?"

I said, "Leg broken and bleeding."

The medic threw a tourniquet to me and told me what to do. It was harder than I thought. I was afraid I was going to cut his leg off with the tourniquet. But the bleeding wouldn't shut down unless we tied the tourniquet tightly. It was such a big vein.

Besides the leg, my driver had a couple of other problems. Shrapnel and pieces of metal had hit him in different parts of his body. And he was burned, too. I could see open burn wounds on his arms.

The military teaches you that you may be wounded, but make sure your brothers aren't wounded worse. Yes, when things are tough, we naturally pause, thinking about our

After hitting an IED, the remains of the shell of the vehicle

Where the metal went through my driver's leg

own wounds, but we also have to consider that others have it worse. It is our duty to push past our hardships and help them.

The platoon was working together in the midst of the chaos. Another Humvee got in position to take interference and guard us. The communications guys were rocking and rolling, alerting the base to make sure they knew we had some guys who needed to be rushed back immediately. We put all the packs in a Humvee that was ready to be the lead car, loaded up the injured guys into another Humvee, and rushed to the hospital.

That last part was probably the scariest, when we realized we've still got to drive the dangerous road to the hospital. The enemy knew where we were and that we were injured. We didn't have much support for the trip. The injured were in the open back of a truck. It was the scariest time in my life. But it doesn't matter; you just do it because it is part of the mission.

It took us only 22 minutes from the blast until those guys were in the hospital getting fixed up. The good thing was everyone lived. One guy had second- and third-degree burns on his hands that required extensive skin care. He had to wear gloves for a long time. Others had shrapnel and glass wounds. Another broke his leg. Some had injuries that they will have to deal with the rest of their lives.

We got tuned up pretty good that day. And that incident brought us together. We made sure everyone got out as quickly as possible. It was the coolest thing to see those guys teaming up, new guys and old guys, all on the same team, working the same program, the same mission.

When we got to the medical facility, I had sustained the

least of the injuries, so I was standing outside. My driver said he wanted to speak to me before going into surgery. I went in and he said, "Hey, brother, I just want to tell you that you saved my life."

That was emotional for me. I started crying. This guy had ridden me hard for being the new guy. But he also knew that I had the same training as he did. Sure, he had more experience in the field, but when we were in crisis, he knew he could rely on me. And he thanked me for it.

> "Never tell people how to do things. Tell them what to do and they will surprise you with their ingenuity."
> —George S. Patton

"Just paying it forward." I told him.

When he went into surgery, I went back outside. But then the burns on my eyes were getting the best of me. My vision was so blurry I could barely see.

I decided I could sit there or make myself useful. I made my way back to base to pick up everybody's gear.

I remember how much my mustache stank. So after I had the gear back in the barracks, I went to shave the mustache off. But I couldn't because it was half burned and the skin underneath was damaged. I gave up with half a mustache and went to the armory.

A few of our guys were there and some from another platoon. One of the guys asked, "Are you the one who went flying out of the turret?"

"Yeah."

He said, "Birdman, gettin' some."

And that's where the name Birdman came from. The name spread like wildfire through the platoon. They said I flew like a bird after getting blown up. Of course, with a last name like Parrott, I'm used to every bird joke thrown my way.

While I wasn't hurt badly, they sent me home for a couple weeks to heal up. When the ordnance rep put my gun and stuff together, he put "Birdman" on the tag. After that, the nickname stuck.

Several guys got kissed by the dragon that day. You're not a hero for fixing your buddy up. We don't go into the service to earn medals; we earn brotherhood, trust, honor. It was a privilege to help my driver because he needed it.

Brotherhood means you ignore your own problems and watch over the people to your right and left. There is that moment where you are aware of yourself and your own injury, but then you recognize that your brother is in even worse danger. You easily and instantly set aside your concerns and focus on others.

The reason you do this is because you know that if the situation were reversed, they would do the same and more for us.

This is why soldiers are uncomfortable receiving medals and official recognition. We know our brothers would do the same and more. We just happened to be the people at that place at that time. I think the medals are more to send a message to other soldiers to make sure they protect their brothers in battle. As a team, as a brotherhood, we each have the same dedication to the mission and the person on our left and right. We go into battle knowing that they have our backs just as we have theirs. We can accomplish so much more with this dedication.

Imagine where America would be as a country if the

citizens had the same dedication to each other. What if we put aside our own selfish concerns and looked after our neighbors, our team, even our family, knowing that they had the same dedication to look after us?

There are certainly heroes who deserve our admiration and respect. Whenever I'm around Sal, I'm inspired to give as much as I can. He serves as a reminder of what is required to serve our fellow man. And that is how he continues to serve his country.

Battery M, 3rd Battalion, 11th Marines, M198 155mm Towed Howitzer south of Baghdad during Operation Iraqi Freedom I, 2003.

Photo by Jud McCrehin, Marine Corps Times, Gannette News.

CHAPTER 4

T.Y.
Iraq

INTRODUCTION:

The first time I met T.Y., I could tell he was a true patriot. T.Y. served as a Marine in Iraq, and he continues to serve his country in government service.

I really got to know T.Y. when an organization he was with wanted to support Sons of the Flag at their golf tournament. They invited me to come to their office to discuss the tournament, our organization, and how we could work together.

I said, "Sure, I'm all about promoting what we are doing to get burn survivors all the attention they deserve."

As our meeting wrapped up, T.Y. said, "Hey, man, can you hold back for a second?"

"Of course."

After everyone left the room, T.Y. got right up in my face, "All right, dude, I want to get more involved."

I said, "Well, what can you do for Sons of the Flag?"

He looked at me with those Marine eyes and said, "What do you got?"

It was the most empowering feeling because it told me right off that he is a Marine. He's proven himself. And now he wants to continue that mission. He wants to help; he just needs something to run with.

You have to understand that T.Y. was an officer, and I was an enlisted man. In the hierarchy of the military, officers don't say, "Let me work for you." But that isn't T.Y. He is so dedicated to mission success that he only wants to serve.

Some people might believe it's reckless to quickly say, "What do you got?" but Sons of the Flag now uses it as our motto. T.Y. is the absolute epitome of motivation. He has helped us take our organization to the next level. We are honored to have him as a part of the team.

When I asked him to represent the Iraq War in our Legacy Jump, he said, "Wow, yeah. I've got to talk about it with my wife first, but for sure, I definitely want to."

I knew he had some reservation because he hadn't jumped out of a plane before. Marines don't typically go to jump school. But I knew he'd join us. Everything that T.Y. has said he wanted to do or tried to do, he has accomplished. T.Y. has incredible integrity.

At our organization we are blessed to have T.Y.'s support. He is one of those Marines who exemplifies what this book is about. At Sons of the Flag, we apply the "T.Y.

method" or "T.Y. effect." When people want to work with us, we look into their eyes and ask, "What can you do for Sons of the Flag?"

If they say something like, "What do you got?" we know they are the types of people we are looking for.

In his chapter, T.Y. doesn't promote what he did in Iraq; instead, he wants us to understand why he served his country. As an officer in the Marine Corps, he was willing to step down from his role and make sure that the boys were taken care of. He put himself in their shoes and asked "How can I help you?" It's not about a certain instance or action, but about what you continually do that matters.

IRAQ:

I grew up in the foothills of rural North Carolina in a home ruled by faith and a work ethic. My father worked in the furniture industry and commuted on a weekly basis from our home to High Point. Later in his career, my father traveled extensively overseas. My mother also worked in the furniture industry while I was young, but became a stay-at-home mom not long after I finished elementary school. I assume that most young men would harbor harsh feelings about their dads not being home. I'm not most young men. I knew from a very early age that my dad was an amazingly dedicated and hard worker. His work ethic and discipline are the things I admire most about him. Needless to say, even now I strive to follow the example he set for me.

I certainly don't want to shortchange my mother's influence. There should be no impression that she was a single parent; my parents were a team. But my dad often was forced to parent via the phone. I suppose the stereotypical picture someone could paint of my mother would be the "sweet little Southern lady who never met a stranger," and while that is extremely accurate, there's just no way to stereotype her. What you need to know most about both of my parents is that they set an unbelievable example for me to follow. From their personal faith in God and tremendous work ethic to their strict parenting, my parents to this day have been the most influential people on any perceived professional and personal success I have had. Their influence is why I chose to serve in the military. No one in my family had served in the military other than my dad's stepfather, with whom I did not have a close relationship, and a distant relative who fought in the Civil War. I chose to serve because of a chain of events that included a higher calling. The influence of my faith and my parents provided me with a calling to serve others and to give my life purpose. I chose to serve simply because that's what I felt God had planned for me.

The pathway to my service and another large influence in this decision was my choice to attend The Citadel, The Military College of South Carolina. The history and tradition of military and public service by Citadel graduates are notable and distinguished. In my mind, there was not a better place to prepare me for serving others. Furthermore, the caliber of individuals attending The Citadel motivated me. One hour into my training as a "knob" (a term of endearment for freshmen at The Citadel) revealed numerous individuals I wanted to emulate, prove myself to, and in essence, serve. Following The Citadel, I knew I wanted to challenge myself in service to others. Obviously I am biased, but I felt there was no greater challenge in serving others than by joining the United States Marine Corps.

Following graduation from The Citadel in 1999, I joined the United States Marine Corps as a second lieutenant. Like all newly commissioned Marine officers, I attended The Basic School (TBS), additional training, and was subsequently stationed at the Marine Corps Air Ground Combat Center (MCAGCC) in 29 Palms, California. I was assigned to the 3rd Battalion, 11th Marines from 2000 to 2003 and served as a guns platoon commander, forward observer, battalion S4-A, battery executive officer, and battery commander. While serving with the 3rd Battalion, 11th Marines, I completed a combat deployment in 2003 for Operation Iraqi Freedom as part of the initial invasion of Iraq.

My first battery commander—a mentor, friend, trusted confidant, and pseudo older brother—had received orders back to The Basic School as a major in mid-2002. During our conversations prior to my deployment to Iraq, he constantly urged me to consider returning to The Basic School for my non-fleet billet (B-billet) tour as an instructor. Like most Marine officers, I had no desire to go back to The Basic School following my time there as a second lieutenant. It was decisively in the rearview mirror. It was an experience I had already had as a student, and it couldn't possibly be any better as an instructor. While it was difficult to admit, the more I talked to him, the more it appealed to me. In hindsight, the appeal was more about spending time and serving with him than it was about being at The Basic School again. It didn't take long for peer pressure to set in, and I amended my wish list of non-fleet tour assignments. The Basic School became my number one choice.

In 2003 during Operation Iraqi Freedom I, my unit pushed across the border of Kuwait as part of the 1st Marine Division's march to Baghdad. I had been frocked (promoted on the collar, not in the wallet) to the rank of captain while in Iraq and subsequently took command of a 155 mm towed howitzer battery just outside Baghdad. Our unit successfully executed its mission; everyone in my unit came home safe. By any measure, I had succeeded as a young Marine officer in the early stages of my career.

Following my deployment to Iraq, I received orders to Quantico, Virginia, and a return to The Basic School. Egotistically, I felt I had a lot to offer as a seasoned company-grade officer fresh off a tour in Iraq. Besides, I was living proof as to why TBS exists. The adage "Every Marine a Rifleman" is ever present at The Basic School. Shortly after I took command of the firing battery, my unit became a provisional infantry company and assisted in securing the southern portions of Baghdad while performing actions that were dubbed Civil Military Operations. Our efforts led to securing and stabilizing our area of operation in southern Baghdad, allowing the Iraqi citizens of that area to attempt to return to a more normal life.

Second lieutenants don't have the luxury of knowing their Military Occupational Specialties (MOS, a.k.a. their jobs) prior to graduating from TBS. There are exceptions for lawyers and pilots. But even lawyers and pilots are mentored and instructed in basic officership, leadership, and more specifically, the basics of infantry and rifle platoon tactics. I was among the first instructors to return to The Basic School having combat experience. On top of that, I had earned command of a unit that transitioned from its primary artillery duties to a traditional infantry company role. Egotistically, my experiences led me to believe that I had what it took to teach and mentor young lieutenants in "the basics" of The Basic School. What I found was that I was categorically out of my league. Despite how much I thought of myself and more so of my experiences, I humbly realized that the "bullpen" (the section of TBS where the instructors work daily) was chock-full of instructors who were clearly superior to me. To this day, the best Marine officers I served with were in the bullpen—men like Todd Bottoms, John Fleming, John Cook, Ian Allen, Brian Chontosh, Todd Widman, Jake Brown, Lee Kuykendall, Paul Beeman—the list is way too long. There is no doubt in my mind that the term "iconic" doesn't do them justice. These men were Marine's Marines. They were polished, savvy, knowledgeable, and more importantly, leaders. Most of these men had combat leadership experience just like me or experiences that well qualified them to teach lieutenants the intangible tools of leadership they would need to succeed as Marine officers. Most impressive was their ability to command the lieutenants' attention. I put a tremendous amount of pressure on myself just to "hang" with my fellow instructors. It was impressive to watch them teach, observe the lieutenants, listen to them, and see the amount of influence we truly had as TBS instructors. For me, part of the answer to the question as to why I served was because of the man to my left and right. In this case, it was because of the instructor to my left and right.

Not long after my assignment as an instructor began, I realized I couldn't afford to screw up. I had to be on my game 100 percent of the time. The lieutenants assigned to The Basic School while I was an instructor needed to understand that not since the Vietnam War had training evolutions, in my opinion, been so important, and even more so was the importance of information we taught them. Shortly after they completed TBS and their MOS school, they would find themselves with their unit preparing for deployments to Iraq or Afghanistan, or both. For me, there was dual accountability. I held myself accountable to the lieutenants to ensure that I conveyed what they needed to know through instruction and also through recounting my own personal mistakes I had made as a lieutenant in hopes they wouldn't make the same ones. And I held myself accountable to my fellow instructors. Words cannot express how impressive my fellow instructors were. To this day I remain humbled by the Marines I served with at TBS. This is also part of my answer to the question as to why I served. Could I compete on the same level as my fellow instructors and be just as good as they were? I dang sure tried. To this day, I still don't feel I held a candle to my fellow instructors. But my efforts to be just as good an instructor as they were hopefully enabled me to serve them, and just as importantly, to serve the lieutenants.

The first company I had the opportunity to actually instruct while I was at TBS was Echo Company 2003. I got to see the early field evolutions and training exercises that they did from basic squad tactics, morphing into platoon tactics, and finishing with company tactics. In one particular field exercise, I was one of the assistant instructors for the instructional evolution of the "Platoon Defense." To keep from boring anyone with the details, in a nutshell, my job in this particular training evolution was to "Socratically" aid the platoon of lieutenants to set up their defense based on the enemy situation that had been provided to them. In this case, the enemy was one of their sister platoons conducting offensive operations against them. Simultaneously, I was critiquing the platoon's overall efforts and to a greater extent evaluating the leadership abilities of the student platoon commander. While there is an emphasis on the student lieutenant making sound tactical decisions during these field training evolutions, there is a greater purpose in using the training evolution as a vehicle to test and evaluate a student lieutenant's leadership capabilities. There is no better evaluation process for leadership than the methodologies of The Basic School. Peer leadership is an equalizer and will separate those who have a God-given natural ability to lead.

I mentioned the fabricated word "Socratically." As instructors, we would often use a method of instruction that would allow the lieutenants to figure things out on their own with small but effective "nudges" from the instructors. But there are certain pieces of the training evolution that you just have to manipulate more than others so the teaching points are made and the lieutenants actually benefit from the training evolution.

On this particular training evolution, the student platoon commander was a second lieutenant named J.P. Blecksmith. When you think of a Marine officer, you picture J.P. He was born to be a Marine officer: a square-jawed, six-foot-plus, 200-pound-plus, chiseled US Naval Academy graduate. He was a beast of a young man. He was confident about his abilities—not arrogant. But he had a presence that can't be taught and certainly can't be learned. He was exceptionally intelligent and had an innate ability to comprehend exactly what you were saying, and more importantly, what you were trying to teach him. Lieutenant Blecksmith had the intangibles required of a Marine officer. He was blessed with leadership that most of his peers were working to achieve. He had a proven mettle above and beyond most of his peers. I don't want to shortchange any of his fellow lieutenants from Echo Company 2003. Their training company was chock-full of promising and capable Marine officers, and Lieutenant Blecksmith was a leader among them. He stood out. And he had stiff competition among his peers. Probably his biggest was from a fellow Naval Academy graduate, Brian Stann, who was equally full of intangibles.

During the Platoon Defense training exercise, Lieutenant Blecksmith formulated his plan, communicated the plan to his platoon (comprised of his fellow lieutenants), and implemented his plan for the defense. He and the student platoon sergeant meticulously ensured everything was prepared and that their fellow lieutenants were executing according to plan. Not surprisingly, Lieutenant Blecksmith had made good tactical decisions based on the intelligence he had been given. He was well prepared, understood the concepts that he'd been learning to this point in the TBS program of instruction, and more importantly, had determined how to effectively communicate to his fellow lieutenants in order to execute this particular training evolution.

As a sidebar, the root of all evil for training evolutions at TBS is land navigation. It is a huge hurdle for the student lieutenants and in turn adds a level of stress and realism to the training evolutions. During the summer and fall, the "Quantico highlands" are thick and often difficult to maneuver through. While this is certainly a tactical advantage for a student platoon in the defense, it can be a crippling variable for the student platoon in the offense. More often than not, the offensive student platoon would stray from their planned route of advance. This required a very deft touch from the instructor accompanying and instructing the offensive platoon. If the offense is off in their land navigation, they may move right past the defense, essentially negating the purpose of the exercise.

Shortly after Lieutenant Blecksmith had his platoon prepared and his defense in position, I received communication from one of my fellow instructors who was teaching and accompanying the offensive platoon. My fellow instructor relayed to me that he wasn't going to be able to correct the offensive platoon's movement and their errors in land navigation and that essentially, they were going to hit Lieutenant Blecksmith's position directly on the back of his defense. As an instructor, another part of my job was to provide updated intelligence on the enemy situation in order to spur the lieutenant into thinking his way through a potential problem that didn't initially exist. In this case, I had to creatively provide Lieutenant Blecksmith with an updated intelligence picture that would enable him to learn, but also enable him to make a decision that would lead to success or failure. I made the decision to try and allow Lieutenant Blecksmith as much of an opportunity as possible to lead and learn. I called Lieutenant Blecksmith over and said, "Two things: First of all, you are a former college football player, right?"

Lieutenant Blecksmith replied, "Yes, sir."

I then said, "Okay, as a quarterback, if you come up to the line of scrimmage after calling your offensive play and you observe something in the defense that could lead to your offensive play being compromised, what do you do?"

Lieutenant Blecksmith immediately said, "I audible, sir."

"Exactly," I said.

I then provided Lieutenant Blecksmith with an intelligence update that led him to believe the enemy had "circumvented additional countermeasures" and they had been observed approaching directly toward the rear of his defense. Without hesitation, Lieutenant Blecksmith jumped up, said, "Got it, sir!" and proceeded to call "an audible" to his plan. J.P. quickly moved from hole to hole, telling his fellow lieutenants who had just spent the better part of six hours preparing fighting positions that they had to adjust everything they had just meticulously and laboriously accomplished. Not only did he move from hole to hole and provide clear and concise adjustments, he did it in less than ten minutes. To this day, I really believe if it had been any other lieutenant, it would not have worked, but because it was J.P., he made sure everyone understood the new plan and could effectively execute it. Not one of the lieutenants questioned his decision. Not one of them second-guessed him. Even in the short timespan they had been together at TBS, he had garnered and earned respect from his peers.

When the offensive platoon began their assault, they were right in the teeth of his defense and the training went off without a hitch. It was a success purely because of J.P. Had he not been able to clearly and calmly think through the situation, not only would the training exercise have been a complete bust, he and his fellow lieutenants wouldn't have learned the valuable lesson of flexibility in planning, a principle that would be crucial to their success when operating in a combat environment.

As their training came to an end, it was bittersweet to see them move on. As an instructor, you get to know them personally while they are students at TBS. You know them by name and face. I remember that even while working with other companies, I often thought about how the lieutenants of Echo 2003 were doing in life after TBS. I kept tabs on several of the lieutenants from that company after they graduated. I knew Lieutenant Blecksmith became an infantry officer and unsurprisingly, had been exceptionally successful during the Infantry Officer Course (IOC). I knew that he would be a phenomenal officer when he reached his fleet assignment. His leadership, morals, and character were impeccable. He was destined for success, and there was no doubt in my mind he would be revered by his Marines as a mentor, teacher, and brother, connections between those who serve that make the brotherhood of military service so strong. What I had not imagined for J.P. Blecksmith were the realities of life and combat.

Following a command formation at TBS, I was made aware that Lieutenant Blecksmith had been killed in action in Iraq on November 11, 2004—Veterans Day.

During Operation Phantom Fury, Fallujah, Iraq, November 2004, Lieutenant Blecksmith was leading the 3rd platoon, India Company, 3rd Battalion, 5th Marines Regiment. India Company 3/5 was one of the first company of Marines to enter the city and start the house-to-house clearing operations in the Jolan District of Fallujah in order to regain a foothold from the insurgents who had taken control of the city. While commanding his platoon during the house-to-house fighting, Lieutenant Blecksmith moved to a rooftop position to better direct one of his squads during the clearing of several buildings in the city. In doing so, he exposed himself to enemy fire and suffered a fatal wound from a sniper. J.P. was being J.P., selflessly thinking about his Marines, trying to put himself in a better position to watch over them, perhaps "call an audible," guide them, and most importantly, keep them safe. He was doing what leaders of Marines do. Operation Phantom Fury resulted in the deaths of over 1,350 insurgent fighters and the regaining of control of the city of Fallujah. Ninety-five Marines were killed in action along with over 1,000 being wounded.

I will never forget that command formation and the feeling I had when I heard his name spoken as a recent TBS graduate who had been killed in action. I broke down on the spot. Looking back on how I felt that day, I realize a great part of my emotions was guilt. I worried and felt a tremendous responsibility that I might not have taught him what I should have, or maybe I had taught him the wrong things. For whatever reason, I felt a tremendous personal responsibility for J.P. I knew that I was just an assistant instructor and wasn't even his Staff Platoon Commander (SPC). But the influence and impact of the staff and the instructors at TBS are tremendous. I was influenced by my SPC and other instructors, and I would be willing to bet that every Marine officer would say the same. As any human being would, I questioned myself. What if I had taught him one more thing or had said something different? Would that have changed the outcome of the events that took J.P.'s life? And that leads me to the closest, most complete answer I can provide as to why I do what I do, why I served, and why I continue to serve.

I want to measure up to men like J.P. Blecksmith. That's what makes me tick. I'm not competing with the superhuman, selfless, and heroic acts on the battlefield. I'm not competing to be better than J.P. or my fellow co-workers. I do what I do (then as a Marine officer and now in my current professional life) just to measure up to the CHARACTER of men like J.P. Blecksmith and the others I serve alongside. There is a constant aspiration to be as good as the man of his caliber and the others that I've mentioned.

It's what keeps me striving to be better. As a Christian, I am called to follow the example of Jesus Christ. I am called to act as Christ acted. This is an impossible task because I'm human. But that doesn't give me the latitude to give up, quit, or not try. I fail...miserably. I fail miserably in my endeavor to be more Christlike, just as I have failed in my endeavor to measure up to men like J.P. But for me, pressing on to achieve the level of character of J.P. Blecksmith or the other men I have served with and the men I continue to serve with strengthens my faith walk. It holds me accountable to the men I aspire to be like and the people I am called to serve.

I believe that is what is unique about the brotherhood of the military and the brotherhood of those serving our country. I feel that we are all trying to aspire to be as good as the examples that are set for us or the men who are to our left and right. Whether it is because of someone who has mentored you, someone you admire, or someone who has provided a legacy for you to follow, that aspiration drives you and keeps you doing what you do. You can't take time off. You can't get tired of aspiring to be like them. You can't quit. As soon as you quit, you've failed them. We are provided the awesome responsibility of being our brothers' keepers. We are responsible for their well-being. If you lose that sense of responsibility, you lose your focus, and you lose the direction and determination that enable you to carry on the legacy of those we are called to serve and those we are called to honor who have paid the ultimate sacrifice.

BIRDMAN:

The military is successful because of its leaders and instructors. I know that I am the man I am today because I had the opportunity to learn from men like T.Y.

In business and politics, so many leaders make it about themselves, not those they serve. And this does a disservice to their team and ultimately their country. Soldiers understand that everyone depends on our leaders. Just listen to the responsibility T.Y. felt for Blecksmith's death. How many leaders in business and politics feel a similar responsibility when their employees face "failure"?

As we started up our first day of BUD/S training, there were around 200 recruits. As time progresses, the class size drops significantly. By Hell Week, men drop like flies. When someone leaves the team, it's a surprise sometimes. Often you know their leaving is good for the team. You want to look at the man next to you and know that you can count on him to get the job done.

Having the instructors grinding on you is the key to successful training. When I'd go through evolutions, I told myself it didn't matter if I got yelled at because I'm going to do what's expected. There is no "try" on the battlefield.

When we'd complete the evolution, the instructors would call us out on what we did and didn't do. With their feedback, we gained confidence that we had what it took because we were working together. Once we are on the battlefield, all we'll have is each other.

I had many great, iconic leaders, especially during training. I think the most impactful were the instructors during BUD/S training. They took us from being snotty brats with more gumption than brains all the way through Hell Week. There is no way I could have made it if it weren't for my instructors.

To be clear, my motivation for making it through Hell Week was that I wanted to hear my mom cry on the phone when I told her I made it. I wanted her to know that all the work raising me had paid off.

When you graduate from Hell Week you get to wear a brown shirt to field training instead of the usual white one. So that's another incentive. You see these guys running around in brown shirts and you know they made it. You want to follow their examples and be better than them. You go harder and harder because you're like, "I want that brown shirt."

It's the little things like that that get you through. You've got to have something to hold on to.

SEAL training is pass/fail; it's not like a job where if you do the minimum, you still get paid. Not everyone receives a ribbon just for showing up. At BUD/S, they want to make sure only the best make it through. If you want to be one of those people in brown shirts, it's up to you to get there. Leaders will inspire you and help you, but in the end, it's up to you.

Yes, they are training your body, but it's not about how fast you run or swim or how strong you are. It's about committing to your teammates and the mission. The leaders are preparing you to be in some heavy situations, and when you are, you won't have time to think about it. You have muscle memory, and when the brain checks out and the muscle memory kicks in, you know exactly what you are supposed to do and you do it on autopilot. This is why such intense training is extremely important.

The last day of Hell Week was particularly tough, not just because our bodies were so beaten down and our minds pushed beyond our limits, but because we still had so much ahead of us. We were still running around with boats on our heads. The instructors told us to drop our boats and face the ocean. We locked arms like we were going to go through surf torture again.

My swim buddy and I locked arms with the men on either side of us. We squinted at each other with blood-shot eyes, ready to go into the surf together. Our bodies were hurting and chafed, but we knew that together we'd be able to do whatever the instructors threw at us. We were

Getting ready to start Hell Week; little did we know I would be the only one of the four still standing one week later.

going to be all right because we had each other.

We were waiting for the command to go out, but the instructors told us to about-face, away from the ocean. When we turned, no one was behind us. The only thing there was a huge American flag at the top of a beach berm.

At that moment, we knew we'd made it. We'd survived Hell Week. We were going to be SEALs. We were going to fight for our country in a manner that only a few have ever or would ever do.

The instructors then ran up from behind the berm and stood behind the flag. The commanding officer raised a megaphone and said, "Congratulations to you future Navy SEALs. Hell Week is secured."

Without any strength left in our cold, beaten-down bodies, we all jumped into the air screaming and hugging and laughing and crying. It was official. We'd made it thanks to our buddies' support, but also because of the guidance and inspiration from our instructors. They pushed us past where we thought we could go, and now they celebrated our victory with us.

When we got back to the barracks, my first order of business was to call my mom. She's the sweetest woman on the face of the earth. She is an angel. She cries at everything.

I was so tired that I just wanted to crash on my bed, but I had to make that phone call. "Hey, Mom!"

She said, "Hey, sweetie. How are you?"

"I'm good, Mom. I'm going to make this short and sweet 'cause I'm really tired, but just want you to know that your boy made it. Your boy made it through Hell Week."

With former Navy SEAL Mark Hayes just after Hell Week

Class 245 finishing medical check after securing Hell Week

My mom and me in front of SEAL Team 7 headquarters

I heard a gasp for air and then faint crying for joy. It was the most satisfying thing I've felt in my life. "Mom, I did it! I'm not a failure anymore. I'm going to make something great of my life."

"I knew you would, Ryan. There wasn't a thought in my mind that you wouldn't succeed. I knew you were going to do it."

I told her, "I'm really tired, and I've got to call Dad really quickly. I will talk with you later. But I did it!"

I hung up and rested my head against the wall for a moment before dialing my dad.

When the phone picked up, I said, "Hey, Dad. Are you there?"

He said, "Yeah, son, yeah. You all right?"

"Is Faye there?" Faye has been my father's life partner since I was seven.

"Yeah."

I said, "Why don't you get her on the phone, too."

When she was on the phone, she said, "Hi, Ry!"

And I said, "Hey, I'm really tired right now, but I want to let you both know that I made it through Hell Week. I did it!"

My dad let out a yell, and Faye started crying. Then Dad said, "Man, I can't believe it. I'm so damn proud of you. Get dressed, Faye. We are going out to celebrate."

With that, I went to bed without a shower or anything.

About two hours later, I woke up briefly to discover my roommate wasn't in his cot. I got up to check on him. He'd fallen asleep in the bath. When I woke him, the water was freezing cold. He let out a yelp and stumbled to bed.

I was so fortunate because when I went through BUD/S, I had some of the most eclectic SEAL instructors. Every single one of them, although older than me, was from a different place, yet all had the same mission.

Because the SEAL community is so small, you end up running into your instructors at different times. You go through their training blocks, and then you won't see them for years at a time or if ever again. But you will always remember them.

And that's what it means to be a great leader. They are as dedicated to you as you are to your mission. They want you to succeed and make sure they give you the skills, mental attitude, and know-how to be successful. While they don't seek praise and recognition, you will always remember them and be thankful for what they've given to you.

Graduating from BUD/S,
November 21, 2003

CHAPTER 5

JOHN WALTERS
9/11

INTRODUCTION:

Johnny Boy is one special cat. He served as a New York firefighter for 14 years. I've got pictures of him as a kid sitting in a little red fire engine wagon. As you'll read, he always wanted to be a firefighter. He worked his way up to one of the elite companies in the fire service.

The interesting thing about Rescue 1's logo is that it is almost identical to the SEAL logo.

What you can't hear in the following pages is John's accent. He's a true New Yorker. He's a real rough-around-the-edges kind of guy. He's the first to show up, to answer the call, and the last one to leave—a true leader.

John was right there at 9/11. He worked at Ground Zero for six months, bringing the bodies of firefighters, police, and civilians back to their families. His company lost 19 members, which was the single greatest loss of life a fire department or any unit ever had up to that day. John has a lot of weight to bear after that terrible day.

After his work at Ground Zero, John continued to serve as a firefighter. He was at a routine call when a taxi driver crashed into the back of the firetruck John was loading, smashing his legs and pinning him to the back of the rig. He was injured beyond belief. His legs were rendered virtually useless in the blink of a eye.

When something like this happens, you can't help but ask, "Why did this happen?" John has truly run the gauntlet. He lost one leg in the accident, crushed the other one, and earlier he was burned in a fire; he's been through hell and back, and today he works full time with Sons of the Flag.

It's an honor to include firefighters in this book because they serve our country every day. After 9/11, they received attention from the media for a few months, but then the attention focused on the military and our continuing fight against terrorism. In the military, when we aren't serving overseas, we are in training or on leave. We aren't engaged in conflict all of the time. But firefighters are engaged every day, especially in firehouses like Rescue 1 and other rescue companies in New York.

Firefighters don't just fight fires, they rescue people and help their communities in all sorts of ways. They are going to endure injuries, burns, and scarring. These guys risk their lives every day to make sure Americans are safe. They are soldiers with a different uniform, especially after 9/11.

This book is not just about the military; it's about service to our country and brotherhood. Firefighters certainly answer the call, and few men display more love for their country and brotherhood than John.

9/11, WALTERS:

I became a firefighter in 1986, but for me it started way before that. I can't remember a point in my life when I didn't want to be a fireman. Some of my early home movies are of me playing firefighter, usually with the help of my cousins and friends. My first birthday party featured fire helmets and a fire truck cake. My father was a member of the Port Washington Fire Department since before I was born, so I guess it was a natural thing to follow in his footsteps.

As a kid, my father would take me to the firehouse on the weekends. I would play with the other "firehouse brats" on the fire trucks.

Some fire departments have what they call a junior fire department. This is where kids between 13 and 17 hang around the firehouse, washing the trucks, and learning about being a firefighter. My dad's firehouse didn't have this program, so I asked him why.

He said, "I don't know." He went to the board of directors and chiefs and said, "We should do this. My son says there's a bunch of people he knows in other towns who have junior fire departments, and we don't have one here."

They said, "You know what? That is a good idea. We will put you in charge of running it."

So I helped the fire department start the program, and I was the first person to join.

I was 20 years old when I lost my buddy Bobby Dayton. He was a volunteer firefighter with us and also a New York City firefighter. His death caused me to learn everything I could about the craft and do the best I could to make sure other firefighters didn't die. I learned that when fire bites you in the ass, it is not biased. It doesn't care if you are paid or not paid, what color you are, or male or female; if it's going to kill you, it's going to kill you.

I studied and trained very hard to learn all I could about our engine company. Eventually, I was elected to be an officer and started moving up the ranks to chief of department.

When I was 24, I took the New York City Fire Department test. I didn't know much about the FDNY other than it was the busiest and largest fire department in the US. It took several years to get hired due to lawsuits and legal action, but eventually I was hired and was sworn in to the FDNY in 1995 with my first cousin Mike Zofchak.

My first firehouse was Engine 237 in Bushwick, Brooklyn. It was started in 1895 and is still housed in the very same firehouse. The guys at Engine 237 took me under their wings and taught me how to be a brother.

I always had my eye on Special Operations, but you don't go into Special Operations until later in your career

> "I have no ambition in this world but one, and that is to be a firefighter. The position may, in the eyes of some, appear to be a lowly one, but we who know the work which the firefighter has to do believe that his is a noble calling....But, above all, our proudest endeavor is to save lives of men—the work of God Himself. Under the impulse of such thoughts, the nobility of the occupation thrills us and stimulates us to deeds of daring, even at the supreme sacrifice.
> —Chief Edward F. Croker, FDNY, circa 1910

because there are so many things to learn. Also, the captain picks who he wants for the company. They want guys who really know what they are doing and are highly motivated. They also want guys with unique skills and who have a good reputation. So you have to work hard and get noticed.

There are seven squad companies and five rescue companies in the FDNY. There are roughly 25 guys in each company, and there are four officers, three lieutenants, and one captain. In all of New York City, there are 12,000 firemen. So you are talking about a small number of people in each rescue or squad company.

Even though it was something that I wanted badly and that I worked hard for, it was tough leaving my firehouse because I was leaving my brothers behind. It's like leaving your family for another family.

I joined Squad Company 288 of the Special Operations Command in 1999. What allowed me to be in an elite company was that I trained my ass off. I was always trying to get better and find a better way to do things. You never know what is going to be thrown at you. But if you are just reactive rather than proactive, you lose. So you train on everything first and foremost.

We were one of the first groups to be trained in terrorism response. They said it was just a matter of time "when," not "if" terrorism would happen. Remember, the World Trade Center had already been bombed once.

When the first attack happened, the chief got on the radio and told the dispatcher that a plane just hit the World Trade Center, and it looked deliberate. That will tell you how much training we'd had. In Manhattan, a plane can hit anything pretty easily, but the chief knew it was intentional. He recognized it for what it was.

I don't like talking about 9/11. It's not something I want to be put on a pedestal for just because I was there. Everybody went to work that day. It wasn't just firemen who died; there were a ton of civilians and police officers and EMTs. Everybody went and did their jobs, and they didn't think twice about it. We did the best we could. Hopefully, in the recovery part of it, we gave some closure to some families at least.

How do you explain it? Everyone who was on duty from my Squad 288 and Rescue 1 was killed. I'm alive because I was off duty when the attacks happened.

Originally, I was supposed to be working on 9/11, but my schedule was changed. On Father's Day in 2001, there had been a fire where three firefighters were killed and a bunch of guys were hurt. So our schedules got switched around and I happened to be off when the attacks happened.

It was a tough time. We went to funeral after funeral after funeral while still working at Ground Zero and the firehouse. To this day, I don't go to church as much as I should because listening to the songs, going to Mass remind me of all those funerals. I wanted to be there for the families and help them with their losses. These were our brothers. You work 24 hours a day with these guys in the firehouse and then they are dead.

I understand that 9/11 is an important part of our national history. Children now learn about it in school. People want to know about it. And I suppose I have some obligation to tell the younger generations.

At the same time, I didn't do anything specific that warrants me being put up on a pedestal, other than the fact that I was there. No one is a firefighter for the accolades or the medals. But when a mother or father is in tears, thanking you for saving their child, you can't put a medal on that.

After 9/11, we went back to work. We rolled our sleeves up and began recruiting new guys to replace the 19 we'd lost. I knew that I'd be leaving the house soon, and I wanted to feel comfortable that the place was up and running the way it should be before I went to Rescue 1 in Manhattan.

It was time to move on. It was a changing of the guard. Younger guys were coming in and some of the older guys I knew were working in Manhattan. It was a career move to work in the most elite company in the world.

Rescue 1 is unlike other firehouses. Most firehouses have a neighborhood, but ours is the whole borough of Manhattan. It's not just fires; we do everything from terrorism to chemical and biological and radiological hazards. People get stuck, entangled, trapped in anything; we're there. If a crane falls down, they call us. Somebody falls in the water, they call us. Somebody gets run over by the subway, they call us. It's a whole host of things, and it's never-ending. Most firehouses have kitchens and the firefighters cook and eat meals together; not us. We mostly did take-out waiting for the next fire or emergency to come our way.

In 2006, I lost my leg in an accident. We were called to take a guy off the railroad tracks. He was a mess. He was so bloody and mangled, it took us some time to save him.

Afterward, we were at the back of the firetruck putting our gear away when this taxi cab crashed into us. Somehow he didn't see the 40-foot-long truck. My legs were crushed between the taxi and the rear bumper of the truck. The accident was so bad that the passengers in the cab had to be hospitalized. I spent two months in the hospital, losing one leg and struggling with severe injuries on the other one.

The thing is, that man that we saved remembered me. After he healed, he came looking for me. His thanks were the best reward I could get for my years of service. At the end of the day, it's not about medals, it's about doing a job that saves lives. It's a true honor and privilege to be able to make that kind of difference in people's lives.

I think at the end of my career, the best thing I can say is that you need to take the time to pass on what others have taught you and what you have learned.

> *"When a man becomes a fireman, his greatest act of bravery has been accomplished. What he does after that is all in the line of work. They were not thinking of getting killed when they went where death lurked. They went there to put the fire out and got killed. Firefighters do not regard themselves as heroes because they do what the business requires.*
> —Chief Edward F. Croker, FDNY, circa 1910
> *speaking upon the death of a deputy chief and four firefighters in February of 1908*

BIRDMAN:

"Everyone wants to be a SEAL on a sunny day," my instructor told me.

Like most kids, I wanted to be a fireman when I grew up. My grandpa was a fireman for 30-plus years. The difference between kids like me and kids like John is that he not only kept pursuing the dream, he continues the dream even after the tragic accident took him away from fire service. He now works with burn survivors as a part of his role with Sons of the Flag.

While we glorify firemen, they face challenges and risks that few Americans would put up with. They serve their communities and nation at personal risk.

Like the SEALs, firemen are not just about all the cool things you see in the movies. Firemen, especially units like Rescue 1 that John belonged to, do much more than fight fires. They are involved in rescues from down in the subways to pulling window washers from the tops of buildings. And they train hard for these different types of rescues.

Few people are aware of the type and intensity of training that firemen and soldiers go through, which reminds me of my training in Kodiak, Alaska.

I'd never traveled anywhere before I went to Kodiak. We showed up in the big bird at an island in the middle of nowhere. The view was incredible, huge mountains all around, bald eagles, bears, beautiful scenery. But it was cold.

As soon as you're settled, you're in the middle of training. You're given new gear, and you have to figure out how to manipulate it. They give you all the dos and don'ts for the training, such as how to deal with animals you might encounter and how to rescue each other when out in the field. The bears were just coming out of hibernation. You must be vigilant in your surroundings because they can get you. They run 30-plus miles an hour uphill, depending on how much you piss them off.

But my first memories were of the cold. It was nearing spring, but still very, very cold.

We did a lot of rappelling, traversing over rivers, over big logs, up mountains, all with a full load of our gear in our packs. You can have 100 pounds of gear on, depending on what you decide to bring. I was new, so I didn't know exactly what we should and should not bring. I began putting everything in and ended up with more than I needed.

There's this one drill called the re-warming drill. It teaches how to get your body back to operating temperature when you're in really cold situations. You strip down to your underwear and sit in water up to your neck for five minutes. The water was ice cold, so needless to say, you

At the top of one of the peaks in Kodiak, Alaska

freeze your balls off. Of course, it's not sunny out, and the wind is blowing.

After five minutes, you move as fast as your frozen body will allow, getting as far away from the water as possible. The thing is, it's so cold outside, you almost want to jump back in the water because it's just a little warmer. You're body is jackhammering. It's painful. You get a horrible headache.

Loaded up with all my gear

Once you go through the drill, you continue your mission. This teaches you to survive no matter the circumstances or conditions. If it were easy, it wouldn't be part of military training.

Crossing rivers is a big part of the training. If you slip and fall into the river with your Kodiak pack on, the pack can pin you under the freezing water. There was this one drill that involved crossing a giant log over a river about 50 feet across...in the rain. They did put a safety officer in the water downstream from the log, just in case.

We had to make it across the wet and slippery log with our loaded pack on. The first three or four guys who tried to cross slipped and fell into the water. We looked at them and thought, "Damn, that sucks," because they have at least 24 hours before we got back to a warm and dry base. They'll be soaking wet and freezing the whole time we're in the field.

Stream crossing in Kodiak, Alaska

The guy before me was a big guy, and he ended up slipping and falling onto the log. But he was strong enough to hang upside down under the log, holding on with a bear hug. He used every muscle, trying to keep from getting wet. Finally his strength ran out and he, too, fell in the water. As much as it sucked for him, it was too damn funny watching him.

Then it was my turn. Sure enough, about three quarters of the way across, the tree started to wobble and my foot slipped. I yelled, "SHIT" and jumped straight in. I thought I'd maybe be knee-deep, but I sank up to my shoulders. My pack was soaked. Not only would I have to wring out all my wet clothes, my pack was even heavier wet. And we had a two-hour hike ahead of us.

My most memorable night was when we were camping on a ridge on top of this beautiful mountain. For some reason I hadn't bothered to waterproof the seams of my tent. And as you can expect, as we started to bed down, huge clouds came rolling in. You could feel the weather change. You could *smell* the temperature drop.

I jumped into my tent, put on my warmies, and tried to sleep.

Well, it started to pour. I was good initially, but that didn't last long as the seams of my tent started to leak. Worse, I had set up my tent in a deer bed, which meant I was in a depression in the ground. As the rain became heavier, water began seeping into the tent, and a puddle began forming around it and under it. I woke up lying in water. Everything was soaked—my gear, my clothes, my sleeping bag, and me.

Right then I got a knock on the tent. It was my turn to take watch. At least I didn't have to open my tent and shut it really quickly to keep it dry because the floor of my tent had already become a small pond.

I spent the next two hours in my wet gear under a bush in the pouring rain. I was miserable. It had to be one of the longest two hours of my life.

When my watch was up, I went back to my tent and it was even more full of water. I pulled everything out, picked up my tent, and dumped all the water out. Of course my teammates heard the commotion. They peeked out of their warm and dry tents to laugh at me.

After the water was out of my tent, I then wrung out my sleeping bag. Back in my tent, I turned on my gas stove full blast, took off all my clothes, and laid them out on the floor along with all my gear. Then I lay down, buck naked, and breathed through the tent zipper so I wasn't inhaling

My tent is the one on the right.

all the fumes. It got super hot in my tent and dried out my equipment. I zoned in and out of sleep for the few hours that remained of the night.

In the morning, we looked like a sorry bunch, especially me. We were huddled under a bush eating breakfast when our instructor said, "Everyone over here."

As an instructor, he didn't have to put himself through the hard times with us. He'd earned the right to wear the Gucci gear and stay warm and comfortable. But here he was, with us, wearing student gear, and just as wet, cold, tired, and miserable as we were. Why? Because he wanted to show us that he was part of the brotherhood. Whatever we were going through, he was there with us. Whatever support we needed, he was ready to offer it. We had lessons to learn, and he wasn't above standing side by side with us as we learned. That's what it means to be a good leader.

We gathered around the fire, and you could just feel his presence as he looked at each one of us before saying, "Boys. Everybody wants to be a SEAL on a sunny day. It's times like these that make us who we are. Granted, you aren't in a gunfight right now, but even getting through this stuff right here makes you a stronger person, a survivor, a team guy."

I looked around at my team. We knew what he was saying was true. When we started on the journey to become elite military commandos, we had certain dreams and expectations. We were a long way from the front lines up there in Alaska. I never thought I'd be freezing my ass off on an island in the middle of nowhere where the closest thing to an enemy we faced was a bear.

Hollywood dramatizes the lives of soldiers. It shows the more glorious moments of kicking in doors and killing the enemy, but what it doesn't show is what it takes to build the kind of person who can be so dedicated to the mission that he will move with his team into a gunfight.

It is similar with firemen, especially the first responders at 9/11. At the time, everyone praised their heroics, but what we didn't see, and no one talked about, was all the hard work that prepared them for this unprecedented event.

And then shortly afterward, the media's attention turned to the war overseas; meanwhile, our firemen were still serving their community.

So when a true patriot like John Walters is brought down while serving, he doesn't get the recognition he deserves for his service. But he continues to serve his nation even with the loss of his leg.

When we look at firemen and soldiers, we overlook the process that prepared them to be the people who they are. They are so dedicated to their mission, they do not draw attention to the preparation and sacrifices they experienced. And soon, too soon, we forget about their accomplishments.

Everyone wants to be a fireman or soldier on a sunny day, but very few suffer through the hardship, rain, and cold days that prepared them to be heroes.

CHAPTER 6

ROB WEIDMANN
9/11

INTRODUCTION:

I was introduced to Rob Weidmann by two Dallas firemen and John Walters. Rob was at Ladder 123 in Crown Heights, New York, when the terrorists hit the Twin Towers. He went on to join Rescue 2, which is one of the most elite fire companies in New York.

The thing about Rescue 1 and Rescue 2 is that not just any fireman can join the team. You have to excel as a fireman before they will even notice you. And then it can still take years before they accept you. It takes a good fireman years to get a shot at one of the New York rescue companies.

Everything that Rob has done has been elite. While he worked as a police officer and at different firehouses, he was constantly working toward getting on Rescue 2. That dedication and perseverance paid off. He achieved what few people have. And for that, he made one hell of a sacrifice.

A few years back, he was injured in a three-story brownstone fire in New York. As you'll read, Rob was trapped and on fire. He went out a window knowing his team would be there to rescue him. When his buddy reached for him, his skin started to come off. It was too painful for Rob, so he pulled himself down the ladder still engulfed in flames.

He was burned over 50 percent of his body. Sons of the Flag is helping him with the surgeries he needs to get back into the fire department. He is undergoing surgery as we write the book.

Rob is one hell of a fireman, one hell of an American. All he wants to do is get back to the guys, the fires, and the gear. Rob decided to join Sons of the Flag to help other burn survivors. He's handed out fliers for us with his hands still in bandages and open wounds on his body. He is the first guy on the floor and the last guy to leave. This seems to be a theme with Rescue Company firemen. He definitely leads from the front.

Rob has run the gauntlet, been burned, dealt with surgeries, but he still serves his country and promotes an organization that can benefit those who suffer like him. The first words out of his mouth are "You need anything?"

9/11, WEIDMANN:

Iremember at a young age, probably four years old, walking into a firehouse with my dad. I will never forget the smell that permeated from the last fire the men had responded to. The big engine and ladder truck, one behind the other, took up most of the floor.

We didn't know anyone there that day, but they welcomed us in for a tour. They let me sit on the engine and bought me a soda. My dad talked to the guys for a bit, and then we left. I had always watched the trucks responding to and returning from alarms, but being in the station that day was impressive.

That's when I knew I wanted to become a firefighter.

When I was a little older, I got a paper route. I started following the sirens on my bicycle. It didn't matter how far I had to go, and most of the time I didn't even have a clue where I was going. Sometimes I couldn't keep up and lost sight of them, but most times I followed them all the way to the location. I watched how they operated and worked together as a team. Whether it was a medical call, helping someone at a critical time, or a structure fire that required hoses and ladders, I was in awe of the brotherhood and dedication of the firefighters.

I became friendly with several firefighters after they started noticing me around. A fire chief invited me to the firehouse on Sunday mornings to volunteer to clean the trucks and spend time with them. Sunday was the day all the firefighters would go to the firehouse for cleaning and maintenance of the rigs. Usually a drill or some kind of training scenario would follow. I was fascinated by the camaraderie these guys had for one another.

I became involved with the junior firefighter program when I turned 14. It was kind of like the Boy Scouts, but we did fire-related activities like learning about the hoses and the ladders, the trucks, and stuff like that. We weren't going to fires, but learning about how to fight them.

On my 18th birthday, I was sworn in to the volunteer fire department as a firefighter. I was so excited to finally get my helmet, boots, and fire coat. I could hardly wait for my first call.

But I wanted to get on the city fire department, and that involved taking the civil service exams, getting everything together, doing the physical and the psychological work, all that crazy stuff.

When all that was finished, I was on the list of guys to hire. By then I was 19 or 20, and there weren't any openings, so I took a police test. As soon as I was 21, I took a job as a cop, even though it wasn't what I really wanted to do.

Finally, two and a half years later, I was called to the fire department. I was ecstatic and could hardly control myself. It was one of the most awesome days I can remember.

I went through the fire academy in May. It is three months long. It's like going to college five days a week for eight hours a day. You're trying to take all the stuff in, taking tests, and studying. They are molding you into something you are going to be for the rest of your life.

As I got closer to graduation, I was able to make some contacts to go to a good station. I didn't want to wind up at a slow station. I wanted a busy pace where I could learn as much as possible and get involved. I wanted the best experience I could get.

It can take months or years to transfer from a slow house to a busier one. Finally, I got a call that I was going to Ladder 123. It was the best news. I don't know why, but I had always wanted to go there. God was looking after me. I felt like I'd won the lottery.

When I walked in the firehouse in 1998, there was no hazing or ball-breaking. It was just, "You are one of us now." This is what I was searching for all my life. When we go out on an emergency, we know the other guys will take responsibility and protect each other. Putting out a fire is a team effort; there's no one person who does it by himself.

I wasn't working on 9/11. That day, I had some time to kill early in the morning, so I went to my old volunteer firehouse, just hanging out. I fell asleep on the couch until my brother called and asked if I'd seen the news about the plane crashing into the tower. I turned on the news and soon after that the other plane hit.

They recalled everybody who was off duty to respond. I immediately dropped all my stuff and drove to my fire-house. It was kind of weird because there was hardly any traffic, almost like I had lights and sirens on my car. I was able to fly through the streets with nobody in the way.

When you come up the Belt Parkway into Brooklyn from Queens, the road rises up like an overpass and you can see the city clearly. I remember seeing all the smoke from the Towers from that point in the road. On the scanner, guys were yelling, everything was going crazy, and the dispatchers were reporting people trapped. It made the hair stand up on the back of my neck. And it still does, so many years later.

I got to the firehouse and everything was chaotic. There were over 50 guys plus retired guys trying to figure out what to do. We got our tools together from the storage locker. One of the lieutenants had a van that we turned into a response vehicle by loading it full of all the extra tools.

We worked for at least 48 hours straight; it could have been as much as 72 hours. It was just a crazy time. Everybody pulled together, and we were there for each other.

My company was lucky; we didn't lose anybody. Guys lost fathers, brothers, cousins, and different relatives and civilians. Another house in our battalion lost all the guys on their truck. We knew them; they were our friends.

I was in Ladder 123 for eight years before I moved to Rescue 2. I knew that Rescue 2 was one of the best fire companies in the world because of what they do. Unlike other companies, they are not limited to a neighborhood. If a situation arises in any of the boroughs, Rescue 2 goes there, whether it be Manhattan or the Bronx or in Queens. When they are done with one emergency, they don't return to the firehouse; instead, they might be taking off to another fire.

When I first approached Rescue 2, I only had three years on the job. They said, "Go back and get another year or two of experience. When you are ready, come back, and we will talk again."

That is what happened. I waited a couple more years

before I contacted the chief to tell him how interested I was. Since Ladder 123 is close to Rescue 2, we often went to the same calls, so they could keep an eye on me and how I was doing. They could see from my actions and how I handled myself at fires that I would be good.

In December 2005, I got to join Rescue 2. It was like I'd hit the lottery again. Everything I'd wanted and looked for, I had accomplished. I was working with senior guys with lots of experience and different backgrounds. They do collapses, diving, fires in the city, car accidents, elevator emergencies, crazy stuff. That is their bread and butter. They have the tools, and they know how to handle situations.

There was so much to learn. You go through a lot of schooling to pass different tests to get certifications on stuff. I was lucky to get the most sought-after positions.

When I first got to Rescue 2, we had an arsonist running around setting things on fire. So we had a lot of work, sometimes six or seven fires in a night.

There's something about being a fireman and helping people. You want to do your job; you don't want to just sleep and watch TV. We like to work out, but ultimately we want to go to fires. Fires are what it's all about for us.

Things changed on December 19, 2011. I had worked the night before, and my wife was running late. I barely had time to say hi and bye to her and my children before I drove off to work. The first night, the 18th, was a regular night. No fires or crazy stuff.

But the next morning at 9 AM everything changed. The bells and whistles went off. There was a fire not too far away with three people trapped. We got our stuff on and jumped on the truck.

When we got there, it wasn't a big deal. There was just a little smoke.

We went to the top floor where the fire was. People were trapped. In both my partner's and my positions, we go toward the front. We knew the fire was in the rear, so we did a quick search in the apartments, shut the doors, and came back to the hallway to wait for the hose line to come up from the engine.

When the water got there, my partner and I hung back in the hallway. We could hear them spraying into the apartment, but we couldn't really see anything. It usually only takes a few minutes to get a fire out. You can knock it all down within a few seconds, but to make sure the fire is out takes more time.

So after the hose came out of the apartment, my partner and I went back in. We began to take the windows out like we normally do to vent the smoke and gasses. Suddenly, I noticed there was some fire over my head. Nothing significant, but we needed to go out to the hallway to regroup.

As we headed back, I saw a fireman at the window. I turned toward him and slapped him on the back to tell him we had to go back to the hallway. With all the smoke, we couldn't see much, so he scooted toward the door in front of me.

Now that I knew I was the last person in the apartment, I began crawling toward the doorway when all of a sudden the whole room lit up. Everything was on fire. The furniture was burning. Ceiling to floor was all in flames. There was no gap in between. And I was on fire.

I remember getting to the wall and feeling along it. I

was basically burning alive, so I needed to get out now. I remember thinking, "If I don't get to the door and get stuck in a closet or another room, I'll be trapped in here." So I went for a window, knowing that no matter what, somebody will see me in the window and lower the aerial ladder toward me or put the bucket up.

So I got myself out of the window, leaning out until they dropped the ladder down to me. I climbed down by myself to the street and waited for EMS.

I'm grateful it was me that got hurt. That was better than if someone else was in there and I didn't see him or her or that I left behind. For me personally, that would have affected me more.

Our job is to protect the firemen. If I failed to help someone out or wasn't able to save them, that would affect me more than if I got burned. I could handle my own injury better than someone else's injury.

Vinny was driving that day. He saw me at the window and lowered the ladder to me.

I relied on him to do his job. He was there for me. He saw I needed help, and he did it without hesitation. If he wasn't there or had left that position, I would have had to wait longer, and who knows what would have happened then.

He yelled at me because I couldn't see the ladder, "Rob, the aerial is right below you. Get on it."

That is brother helping brother. I might have helped the other guy get out of the room, but Vinny helped me out of the fire.

I knew I was burned, but not how badly. Sixty percent of

my body was burned with third-degree burns throughout. My back, shoulder, and both legs were the worst. When I was in the window, I was leaning out as far as I could so my right side got worse burns.

When I got to the hospital, they redirected a chief to be there with me. I'd known him since I was a little kid chasing fire trucks. He helped guide me into the brotherhood.

The chief met me at the hospital. He said I didn't have to worry about making calls. They picked up my wife from work and drove her into the city. They took care of my parents and my kids. There was always one guy on watch with my family. My wife always had someone to pick her up in the morning and drop her off at night.

The first couple of weeks I was in an induced coma. When I first got to the emergency room, I remember them giving me something, and I remember being rolled out of that room to the elevators and seeing the chief and shrugging my shoulders.

The hospital people told me they were going to induce me, and I don't remember anything for the next couple of weeks. I didn't think it was going to be that long. When I woke up, my wife told me I'd been in a coma for two weeks. I thought it was only a day or two.

During the next few months in the hospital, a different firehouse would cook for my family. The commissioner checked on me often. Guys from different firehouses would visit me. These guys were sacrificing time from their own families to help my family. It was only a couple of days before Christmas and my wife would tell them to go home and be with their families. She'd say, "Rob wouldn't want you to be here when you should be with your family."

When I was finally able to leave after three and a half

months, it was an incredible send-off.

First, I was asked to be on television. I'm not really into that; I just do my thing. But it was a way for me to thank everyone who helped out.

When I walked into the room, there were all these cameras. There was also a shitload of guys from the fire department who applauded. It was overwhelming. I wasn't expecting it.

After the interview, the whole way out of the hospital was lined with guys, shoulder to shoulder.

When we left the hospital, men were still shoulder to shoulder, three deep, all the way to the parking area. I got a police escort from the state troopers. There was a fire boat in the East River shooting water cannons, and a sign saying, "Welcome Home, Brother."

I remember Rescue 4 in Queens gave us an escort to the border of the county. Along the way, there were fire companies lined up on the side of the road and on overpasses. The guys would either be on top of the rigs saluting or beside the rigs with flags. It was unbelievable.

I wish I had prepared for the whole thing. I would have recorded it because it would have been something to hold on to forever.

When we got to my town, there were tower ladders set up with American flags on both corners of my block. From one corner to the next, there were more than a hundred people lined up, and our car was escorted by the state troopers. Everyone was clapping and cheering.

I never saw anything quite like it before and have never seen anything like it since. It was an incredible welcome home.

Over the years, I never forgot my first firehouse visit

and my desire to join the ranks of the FDNY. Each firehouse and fire department is unique with its own history and traditions. How that history and those traditions carry on and new ones are made depend on the members.

In the late 1800s, an FDNY fire chief gave a speech turned poem that is very well known to firefighters. The poem was named, To Be A Fireman, by Edward F. Croker.

I have no ambition in this world but one, and that is to be a fireman. The position may, in the eyes of some, appear to be a lowly one; but we who know the work which a fireman has to do, believe that his is a noble calling.

We strive to preserve from destruction the wealth of the world, which is the product of the industry of men, necessary for the comfort of both the rich and the poor. We are the defenders from fire of the art which has beautified the world, the product of the genius of men, and the means or the refinement of mankind.

But above all, our proudest endeavor is to save the lives of men—the work of God Himself.

Under the impulse of such thoughts, the nobility of the occupation thrills us and stimulates us to deeds of daring, even at the supreme sacrifice. Such considerations may not strike the average mind, but they are sufficient to fill the limit of our ambition in life and to make us serve the general purpose of human society.
—Chief Edward F. Croker, FDNY

These words still hold strong and true today. They continue to inspire me, as they will future firefighters.

There is a lifelong bond that firefighters have for one another. The meaning of brotherhood is much deeper than anyone outside the fire service can truly understand. This brotherhood we share is forged by the selfless sacrifices we make for one another. These sacrifices result in thousands of severe injuries and hundreds of deaths to our brothers every year. One minute you may be sitting around a table joking, breaking each other's chops, then, in a matter of seconds, you're on your feet to a major incident where one of us may not return. In the bad times, our brothers will comfort and care for us and our families. The brothers are always there, no matter what.

The extraordinary commitment, dedication, courage, loyalty, and respect that firefighters have is incomparable to any other brotherhood I know of. Our love for our job and each other, both on and off duty, is immeasurable. I am grateful and honored to be part of the "bravest" firefighters!

BIRDMAN:

When Rob went out that window, he knew his brothers would save him. It's not just about doing their jobs; they do it because of their dedication to and respect for each other. That sense of trust in your brothers comes from training together, eating together, bleeding together, and finishing together. Everything is a team effort.

On my first deployment in Iraq, I knew I still had a lot to learn. As a new guy, I hadn't seen the evils of war yet, so I turned to my teammates. Simply wearing my trident or a platoon patch doesn't cut it. You're always the new guy to someone.

I had just gotten to Iraq and was sitting in a little room with this guy from another SEAL team. One of the other guys mentioned that this guy had a large number of lethal shots as a sniper.

"Holy cow," I thought. "I'm sitting next to a proven shooter, a guy who has been there and seen the show." I couldn't help myself; I asked him point blank, "I'm a new guy. I've never done this before. What's it like in combat?"

He just smiled. Chris Kyle was humble and quiet; he was all about the boys. When his team got asked to do a mission, there was no argument out of him.

Chris was one of those iconic guys who found himself in the right place at the right time. Snipers have to be smarter than the terrorists, not just in shooting, but in many other tricks that American snipers are trained to do. When Chris was given the chance and opportunity to make those shots and be in those positions, he took them. He worked hard to be an expert at his craft.

I looked up to Chris Kyle and idolized him. No matter what job you do, you idolize those who have succeeded in a big way. They will show you what can be done and how

On patrol in Iraq

to do it better. Chris was a true American patriot and hero. I recommend you read his book, *American Sniper: The Autobiography of the Most Lethal Sniper in US Military History.*

Chris gave me some of the tools I needed to become a stronger SEAL. I was honored to serve with Chris even though we were never in combat together. I will always love you, brother. I'll never forget. You are "the legend."

When you first join a platoon, they find out who you are, where you come from, what you've done, different attributes and characteristics about you, and what your skills are. If you were a hunter, maybe you'd be an ordnance rep and be in charge of all the weapons. If you are a really sharp cat, you might go into intel. If you were a truck or car guy and know how to work on engines, you might be a first lieutenant who works with motors. There are only a dozen or so of us in a platoon, so we each have a specific job.

When I first joined my platoon, there were two jobs available, coms and ordnance reps. The other new guy had gotten through BUD/S a couple months before me, so he got to choose first.

He asked for ordnance, and they immediately turned it around on him and gave him coms. It doesn't matter what job you get, you crush it, not because you want the status or recognition, but because if you're not your best, you can get someone killed.

So I got ordnance rep, which meant I worked in the armory. I had to know everything there was about the weapons and gear. The former ordnance rep taught me everything I needed to know before he went on to sniper school. Even at sniper school, one of the toughest training programs, he continued to check on me to make sure I was doing things right and getting the weapons ready for our team. I learned how to manipulate weapons, the symptoms of malfunctions, and anything else I would need to keep the weapons in perfect shape for our team.

You not only have to learn your job, you have to also learn everybody else's because it's very possible that they are going to get hurt, killed, fill some other role, or transition out of the platoon, and you'll need to pick up the slack. SEALs are unique individuals who become the jack-of-all-

trades. They are competent in most areas, but seldom experts at anything except their assigned roles on the team.

Over time, as you become a better operator, you get more proficient. Some of the older guys I learned from were so calm and collected during the chaos. They viewed every situation logically. They taught me that compartmentalization pushes all the foolish, annoying stuff to the side when there's chaos. Then you can focus on the mission.

Even in civilian life, we often get stressed out by things we can't control. The situation is the situation; we need to focus on the mission.

The interesting thing about SEAL training is that you have peer evaluations. Your team ranks you on how well you work with others and if they like you. That way, you always know how you are sitting on the team. If you get a bad peer evaluation, your instructor is going to sit down with you.

Corporations don't do this nearly enough. They are too

SEAL headquarters in Iraq, former Saddam Hussein Palace

politically correct and fail to hold people to a standard. The reason firemen and soldiers are so good is we have a standard that we stick to. If there is no standard or if companies don't uphold their standards, they are going to fail. But if you keep the standard and your team exceeds the standard, you're going to crush it.

In business, if you screw up, you might get a write-up or no pay increase, but for firemen and soldiers, it's pass/fail. If you don't meet the standard and you fail, you're done. You're out. Or worst of all, someone gets killed.

In BUD/S training, they start with over 150 guys and graduate only around 40. Instructors only want the best guys on their teams. You are tested on everything, and if you don't cut the standard, you are gone.

Let's say in your physical readiness test the minimum is 100 push-ups in two minutes, 100 sit-ups in two minutes, and a 1.5-mile run in nine minutes. A SEAL doesn't just want to complete the standard, he wants to crush it. It is not good enough to be average.

And I know that firemen at Rob's level have that same self-motivation. They don't even think about self-fulfillment because they are serving something so much greater and at such a bigger magnitude.

When you're doing something greater than yourself, you can't go wrong. Firemen don't get paid a bonus for going out on very risky operations. Soldiers don't get more recognition when they attack a high-value target than when they are simply protecting a village. But we all stay ready and motivated to go way beyond what is expected.

CHAPTER 7

TOM BUNING
Desert Storm

INTRODUCTION:

When I was looking for a jumper to represent Desert Storm, I had a problem. I talked with vet after vet and couldn't find a candidate who served in Desert Storm. Finally, someone said, "I know a guy. He's the associate athletic director at SMU (Southern Methodist University in Dallas, Texas)."

When I was put in touch with Tom Buning, I told him about what we do at Sons of the Flag and that we would like him to be on our jump team to represent Desert Storm.

Without any reservation he said, "I'm in."

I thought Tom was just another soldier with a couple years of service, but it turned out that he was a lieutenant colonel who served for 24 years.

I stayed in touch with Tom in the months leading up to the jump to keep him in the loop, getting his medical records, and so on. It wasn't until the jump that I actually met him in person. I'd seen pictures of him, so I introduced myself to him, "Hey, I'm Birdman."

With a big grin on his face, he said, "Birdman! I'm Tom Buning."

I said, "Awesome! Are you ready to fly the sky today?"

And he said, "Oh, I'm ready."

His perspective on being a leader is very important because it takes all different types to make the military what it is—guys like Tom and our predecessors who gave us the tools we use as servicemen. The only reason we are able to do what we do is because of the people who have done it before and led us. All these guys are part of the legacy that builds us up to be the soldiers we are today.

After the jump, Tom came to me and said, "Whatever you need from me, I'm in." And so he continues to serve his country.

DESERT STORM:

Even though I knew my father had been in the Army during World War II, he never spoke about it. Besides a picture on the wall of him in uniform, I recall two other reminders of his combat duty during my childhood.

The first was my father would sweat in his air conditioned office. We had a big family with eight kids and lived in Orlando, Florida, in a large house with no air conditioning. We didn't have much money, so there were only two places with window A/C units in the house: my dad's two-room insurance office at the front of the house and my parents' bedroom. When I had the chance to visit him in the office, I noticed that he would have drops of water running down the sides of his face from his hairline. When I asked him how he could sweat sitting in such a cool room, I was told it was from being shot in the war. (He had been shot through the cheek—the bullet exiting the back of his neck, nicking the nerve that regulated his sweat gland.)

The second reminder of his service was the scar from that bullet. Kissing him good night, I'd see the dimple the bullet left behind.

The details are sketchy, but my dad went into Germany about a month after D-Day. An infantry first lieutenant in command of a platoon, he was wounded in action and stayed in theater. Once he was healthy, he joined another Army unit to keep fighting until the end of the war.

My older brother, Richard, graduated from high school and joined the Marines in 1968 during the middle of the Vietnam War. At that point, I had never been out of Florida, but the whole family went to Parris Island for his graduation. I remember feeling excited because everyone there had the same 25-cent, barber haircut as my younger brother and me.

My brother's service during the war became a part of our family life. I remember sending him care packages, adding my hello to the audio tapes that we would send him, and listening to the tapes we received from him. We were very proud of Richard, missed him dearly, and made him a part of our daily prayers.

My father had always been patriotic, but as I got older, I began to notice how important his country was to him. He taught me dedication and perseverance. At the YMCA, I applied these traits to swimming, a sport I enjoyed and improved at quickly. I knew that my parents couldn't afford college, so I worked hard to be the best student and swimmer possible to get a scholarship.

One day, my dad brought home some information about the Coast Guard and the Naval academies. Out of respect, I went through the admissions process, but my application seemed to go into limbo.

My sister, who was working as an assistant swim coach at the time, found a brochure for Army swimming and brought it home for me to fill out. I looked into things a bit, and I learned that other good swimmers I respected had gotten into West Point. In just a short time, I was being called by the Army swimming coach, and the next thing I knew, I had the nomination and an appointment.

The first time I was ever on a plane, I traveled by myself to West Point.

West Point lived up to its billing. I was struck immediately by the talent and caliber of the people I was with. I thought, "These are people I want to be around." Beyond being smart and athletic, their other talents were unbelievable. For me, it was like winning the sweepstakes. I loved learning, and this was a nonstop opportunity.

After graduating from West Point, I completed the Engineer Officer Basic Course and went to Ranger School before shipping out to my first assignment in Germany. I served for two years as an engineer platoon leader in the Third Armored Division before returning to the States for a special assignment. In an extraordinary move, the Army was allowing me to pursue my passion and realize my athletic potential by assigning me to the US Modern Pentathlon Training Center at Fort Sam Houston, San Antonio,Texas. I was able to join the world-class athlete program for four years in the five-sport discipline of riding, fencing, swimming, shooting, and running. An Olympic sport with a military tradition, it debuted in the 1912 games when First Lieutenant George S. Patton represented the USA. My goal was to make the four-man 1988 Olympic team.

Having finished fourth in the US Nationals in 1987, I became part of an elite US training squad that traveled the world to participate in World Cup competitions in preparation for the trials and Olympics. With the loving support of my wife, Debi, an Air Force brat and daughter of a four-star general, achieving my audacious goals was becoming a reality.

Unfortunately, one bad event at the Olympic trials overshadowed great performances in the other four. No excuses; I gave it my best. I was thrilled to have the chance to compete and represent the USA, especially on trips to the Soviet Union and other Eastern Bloc countries. Once again, I benefited from an educational experience that couldn't be duplicated in a classroom.

Calling "end of mission" to my internationally competitive career, I phoned my assignments officer and said, "Send me back to the troops."

From that point on, I knew that I had to invest myself tenfold back into my career. In the best shape of my life and highly motivated to pay back the Army for allowing me to pursue my athletic dreams—I knew I could do it! With orders in hand, Debi and I packed for Europe.

By the time I arrived back in Germany, I was an older captain who had yet to serve as a company commander —a mandatory requirement for career progression. Within a year in Germany, I took command of Headquarters and Headquarters Company of the Third Armored Division's 23rd Engineer Battalion. The largest of six companies, I was now responsible for over 180 men located in satellite units in four different German communities and a very large organization right under the flagpole.

In November 1990, we were completing our last major training exercise of the year at the Combat Maneuver Training Center at Grafenwoehr. I was approaching the 18th month in command, a typical milestone when leaders are changed to maintain a steady rotation of captains into command assignments. In fact, an official date for the ceremony was on the battalion's training calendar.

Upon our return from the field to the barracks, we were told that there would be a major announcement on *CNN* later that evening from General Colin Powell. We gathered around the television as the general announced that in response to failed negotiations with Saddam Hussein to remove Iraqi forces from Kuwait, the United States was changing its defensive posture to an offensive capability by deploying two armored divisions from the States and two more from Germany to the Middle East as part of Operation Desert Shield.

We all looked at each other, jaws agape. Wait, there were only two armored divisions in Germany, and we're one of them!

More interestingly, those two divisions hadn't been out of Germany since World War II. We had trained for the same Cold War mission for nearly 50 years; defend Europe from a Soviet invasion and hold the defense at all costs until stateside forces could deploy as reinforcements. Our training involved preparation to roll out of the gates at a moment's notice, driving tanks on the highways to secure key terrain along the East-West German border. Deployments were only a necessary part of getting to Germany's maneuver training area. This involved putting equipment on a combination of flatbed railcars and semitrailers, and our troops on buses.

By Thanksgiving we had unit deployment orders and personnel stop loss was in effect, freezing all leaders in their positions and canceling the scheduled individual rotation to other duty stations or discharge from the Army.

As the commander of a well-seasoned team, I was now responsible for deploying my company to a combat zone. This time it was all different. They told us to take what we needed and to plan on being gone for a year, and most importantly, be combat ready.

This time, tanks were put on trains and shipped to ports. Our division, over 10,000 strong, moved all its equipment across oceans and seas to not just another country, but another continent.

We had no concept of how to deploy across great distances. We were used to a situation where when you forgot something, you would simply drive an hour or so back to base and get it. Now we were loading up and expecting to stay away for an extended period. Trading the hills, valleys, farmland, and forests of Germany for the deserts of the Middle East, we had crash courses in everything from maneuver warfare to personal hygiene.

Once our equipment was shipped, we had two weeks to focus on our personal lives. Debi and I were the proud parents of Chase, our six-month-old son. Our previous plans for a trip home to see family, a baptism, and some well-deserved vacation were put on hold; instead, we rushed to have Chase baptized. We had only days to organize all the other important details like wills and medical instructions. There were medical checks, lots of immunizations, and even dental work needed to get done.

Two weeks later, we boarded planes for Saudi Arabia and the ramp-up from Desert Shield to Desert Storm. Arriving in mid-December, Christmas would be spent in Saudi Arabia.

When we landed in theater, our first mission was defense of Saudi Arabia. Immediately after we got our equipment collected at the port, we moved out into the assembly areas in the desert. Everything was different; for instance, there was the contrast of our green tanks and woodland camouflage uniforms against the desert sand.

Focus and urgency were the orders of the day as we prepared for the deadline for Saddam Hussein to leave Kuwait, which was rapidly approaching.

When the deadline passed without a response from Iraq, we commenced with a relentless air war, which went on for about 30 days. We didn't know what the Iraq response would be, so we were in full planning and preparation with British and French armored divisions along with the US Army's Seventh Corps. This massive armored force was the largest battle command assembled since World War II.

We moved out quietly into the desert along the Iraq border, far west of Kuwait. We reached a position that allowed for a surprise flanking attack against the elite Iraqi Republican Guard, who were oriented on Kuwait to defend against a likely US-led coalition attack from the east through Kuwait.

Through daily contacts with my men, I found some of them had become fixated on listening to the radio news broadcast hourly by Armed Forces Network. With the air war underway and no signs of an Iraqi willingness to leave Kuwait, the soldiers hung on every word, asking, "What does this mean? Are we going to war?" It was amazing how much strength people gave each other. When someone started to worry, someone else would be there for support. Confidence in our training, equipment, and teammates kept our stress reactions down.

Then the day came to deploy. Attached to the lead brigade of the Third Armored Division which led a five-division main attack force on the Iraqi Republican Guard meant we were first across the line of departure. As engineers, we had a significant role upfront to provide mobility and countermobility. We faced significant obstacles that needed to be destroyed or quickly overcome. For instance, we deployed assault bridges over ravines to make as level a road as possible. Perhaps our biggest and most stressful job was de-mining. Our nightmare was the possibility that a mine would not only cause a major slowdown, but there also might be a loss of life.

We moved into enemy territory at night. As daybreak came, our movement brought us to our first encounter with Iraqi reserve forces. The air war had decimated their units and equipment, and with lines of supply cut off for weeks, they were clearly emaciated and starving. Our first big problem was that they wanted to surrender *en masse* and we couldn't stop beyond making sure they were un-armed.

We continued moving in combat formation. Tanks covered the desert as far as you could see. With the weather deteriorating into dusty wind, rain, and fog, we pressed on.

Although we traveled night and day, there were periods when we'd stop. If we didn't know how long we would be stopping for, we had to prepare for incoming fire. Together we'd dig a hole next to our vehicles in case we needed to jump into them for protection. Even a quick nap was taken in a hole with your nose inches below the ground.

One night I heard an explosion at the back of the column. My first thought was that someone had misfired a weapon, hit a mine, or set off an unexploded ordnance dropped during the air war.

About 10 minutes later, we realized that we were actually engaging the enemy. That first round was fired to register in on the enemy. It was followed shortly by hundreds of artillery rounds with multiple warheads that blanketed a whole square kilometer.

As fast as it started, it was over. It took a hundred hours by most counts to render the Republican Guard ineffective. The Iraqis had suffered some through the air war, but they were still ready to fight. Luckily, all the realistic training using our superior weapons systems allowed us to not only see the enemy first, but we were also able to engage them at a further distance than they could fire. Even when we discovered them at close range, our crews were able to react with superior teamwork. As a result, we were able to win with very minimal losses. Our few losses were sad, but compared to how many were standing at the end of the day, it was miraculous.

When the sun came up, we had our cease-fire orders and used the time to secure our areas, sweeping and clearing out Iraqi positions, dismantling their equipment, and destroying ammunition caches.

My driver, Specialist Rogers, and I were on the ground inspecting an area where an Iraqi armored force had headquartered. We found damaged vehicles in fighting positions and some well-thought-out underground protective bunkers. I surprised who I thought was a single Iraqi soldier in an underground bunker. As I yelled to Rogers to quickly provide reinforcement, the startled Iraqi came out of the bunker, hands in the air.

My weapon drawn and aimed at this POW, I yelled even louder for Rogers, who hadn't heard the first call. The Iraqi soldier's actions got more frantic as he pointed down into the bunker he had come out of.

As I looked down into the hole, I saw more soldiers were starting to climb up and out of it. Armed only with my .45

pistol, I began to count the enemy soldiers until they numbered seven—the exact number of bullets in the magazine. The marksmanship skills honed in years of nerve-racking international competition as a pentathlete gave me some needed confidence.

After what seemed like an eternity, Rogers arrived with his rifle at the ready, helped spread the POWs apart from each other, and searched them while I kept him covered.

The POWs were eventually released to the military police, who moved them to holding areas. I was briefed later by an interpreter that the Iraqis had feared for their lives because of my yelling. I was glad they didn't know what "Rogers" meant!

Once our area was secured, we went into standby mode, waiting to find out what the status of the potential peace negotiations was.

And that's when a whole set of new problems began. Iraqi forces leaving Kuwait in clear violation of our rules were trying to take their combat equipment with them. With our forces located along that highway between them and Baghdad, there was more work to be done. Of course we didn't let them pass.

For the tanks, it was a little like a shooting arcade. For the engineers, we used our expertise with explosives to destroy any salvageable weapons systems or ammunition.

Over time, we transitioned to peace enforcement and some refuge control. Limited by mission orders, continuing the fight onto Baghdad was not a possibility. At night, we could hear the distant gunfire of Iraqi forces seeking their revenge on dissident factions within their own country. The days would be filled with growing numbers of refugees seeking food and shelter.

In my short time in combat, I realized how important the team is. As an athlete, I'd spent most of my time as a swimmer, which is mostly an individual sport. Yes, you excel individually, but you can also add your points to your teammates' and form relays to win a team trophy. There was always a great sense of excitement as we prepared for a big championship; you just had to figure out how to get the payoff.

For me, it was the same with the military. We had to succeed individually for the good of the team. But in this case, there weren't trophies; instead, we completed the mission and returned home.

Once our forces were consolidated back in Kuwait, everyone wanted to know one thing: "When can we go back home?"

At the time, the United States Army was trying to figure out what it was going to do with its Germany-based divisions now that the Cold War was over and the Wall was down. More time was needed to figure that out; plus, our engineering skills and talents were needed in Kuwait. So we moved to the bottom of the redeployment list, and our unit stayed the longest.

We worked on restoring Kuwait's infrastructure and securing a home for US combat forces because Saddam Hussein remained in power and could act up again.

But the soldiers' minds were elsewhere. They were getting homesick. Since I'm a physical fitness guy, I used sports to get their minds off what they couldn't change. We fired up our bulldozers and built a makeshift sports field. We pushed up sand berms to form a rectangular field and used some old camouflage nets and steel frames to make goals. We had a miniature soccer field.

Every morning, we played a new game that involved one team getting something past a goalie into a net. It could be a frisbee, volleyball, soccer ball, you name it. And every game was done with the burning oil wells in the distance, their flames shooting so high they could be seen for miles. The solid sky of black smoke cast a dark haze.

When the men would pause for some water, they would spit or clear their noses, and you could clearly see the specks of charcoal they had breathed in. But they were having too much fun to care. The games were a great stress buster.

Of course, we also needed showers with all the sweat and smoke. So we used that great engineering know-how and our mechanics' machine shop to build stands to hold up big tanks of water with a drawstring valve leading to a showerhead. We painted the tanks black. By the end of the day, the water was good and hot.

All this activity built morale along with the knowledge that we were part of the winning team. We had some non-combat-related accidents that, unfortunately, happen when you combine long hours, men, and machinery. Others discovered genetic health issues or had to deal with chronic conditions that flared up on occasion. But what a blessing it is to say, "I brought everyone back." For that, I'm eternally blessed.

When we finally did get to go back to Germany, a change of command date was set. I ended up being a company commander for almost twice the time that somebody normally would. It was a defining time in my life and professional career. It was also the most rewarding experience on so many levels.

My command philosophy was to make sure everyone knew the bigger picture as well as the details of their jobs. Some folks were always talking about what we were doing tomorrow, but I made sure they knew the big picture and kept an eye on the horizon. It was also important to let everyone know that no matter how split up our unit became, we were still one team.

I remember taking time out to say a prayer with one of our support sections as they departed to link up with the unit they would support. It seemed natural at the time, and I think everybody felt the same. As for results, those prayers were all answered.

In the end, we can only do our best to serve our team and our country. Whatever I can do to serve, pass on, or help—that's what's important. It's not about me; it's about the next guy. We're dedicated to a mission.

In my case and in my experience, we faced an interesting war in a manner that had been untested. We did our best. My responsibility was to bring my men safely home. And I succeeded, but not because of something special about me. I had been given training and opportunity as had my troops. Everyone had a job to do. They were trained, they were dedicated, and they completed their mission. Nothing can be better than that.

BIRDMAN:

I'm inspired by Tom's perspective. As an engineer and a lieutenant colonel, his perspective of war and mission is much different than mine. For me as a soldier, I was responsible for getting my buddies from here to there, to make sure I was in position and ready to fight. Tom had to move whole companies and make sure the logistics were sound and that his men had what they needed, when they needed it.

As an enlisted man, I received orders down the chain of command from leaders like Tom. Often, it was up to us to find a way to meet the objective once we were in the field.

I think the best example of this was when I was in sniper school, and how I got there is an interesting story...

Old Blue was a sniper on our team. I looked up to him, thinking how humble and quiet he was. He would teach me about ballistics, about the effect of the spin drift of the earth, and so on. And I was thinking how intriguing all this was. I asked him what it takes to be a sniper and how I could become one.

Old Blue told me that sniper school is the toughest school in the teams. Even the toughest elite operators struggled at sniper school.

His words and example inspired me. I let my chief know that I wanted to go to sniper school, and without hesitation, he enrolled me.

Now, sniper school isn't something that you just put your name in and get. There is a waiting list. There is a small group of students in the class, so only a few guys are let in.

The program is about more than just shooting. You have to understand concealment, evasion, and infiltration. We turn ourselves into the ground, trying to evade the enemy while we move closer to the target.

When you're stalking, you don't have two-man teams like you do in most of your operations. It's just you, by yourself, stalking.

Being isolated makes a SEAL uneasy because from the beginning of SEAL training you always have your swim buddy. Now you are out there on your own, feeling extremely exposed. No one has your back.

Sighting in on a target

For one assignment, I thought I would go a different way toward the target. I located a little channel of eight-foot-high cattails and ankle-deep water that got deeper and deeper as I approached the target. I could actually run through the channel and get to the target a lot quicker; after all, I only had four hours to stalk, reach the target, and set up.

As I got closer to the target, I slowed my pace, knowing I had enough time. I just needed to climb a little hill. But before I climbed, I turned myself into a bush.

All of a sudden, my buddy's head popped out of the other side of a bush that was about 25 feet above me. "Hey," he

In the armory in Iraq with my "pig" (MK 48)

said.

I started laughing because all I could see was a freaking bush with a sweaty and camouflaged face looking at me! He had crawled the whole way to the hill.

He said, "Man, this is an ass-kicker." He was older than me, mid-30s. "I don't have a good shot. I'm coming down," he said, and threw his rucksack down next to me. Then he jumped.

Now, this guy is six foot two inches, maybe 215 pounds. There's no way I'm going to catch him. But he launched into a front flip. While I watched, I thought, "This dude is fully committed."

He came down right on top of me and we both landed hard on the ground. It was like a comedy where, if you're watching it, you laugh, but if you're on the receiving end, it just plain sucks. There we were, both lying on the ground in pain, but at least we were safe and the instructor didn't see us.

When the pain went away, we started laughing.

Then he asked, "Dude, have you seen the target?"

I nodded, "We're in perfect position." Getting in a good position is the hard part. Shooting the target is much easier because we are trained to shoot precisely.

We both passed that day. We could stand together and laugh about the parts we'd messed up because we both made it to the finish line. That is what builds camaraderie and brotherhood, being able to stand on each other's left and right and laugh about the hard times and tell everyone how we made it.

What Hollywood doesn't show about a mission is that it never goes as planned. As soldiers, we are trained to deviate on the fly with speed, ensuring that everybody is going to come back.

When sniper school was completed, they had Medal of Honor recipient Sammy L. Davis, retired United States Army Sergeant First Class, give us our certificates. He shared with us what it means to sacrifice for your country. Like many Medal of Honor recipients, he had a sense of loss because he received the medal during a horrible conflict where some of his brothers did not return. You know that he has done something unbelievable, but for him, he's a regular soldier, a regular guy. What an honor to finish sniper school with Mr. Davis standing by our sides.

When I returned to my platoon as a sniper, I got my

Doing overwatch for the Marines as they pushed through Ramadi

own outfit of rifles. Just looking at the rifles and putting your name on them is empowering. That puts you into overdrive. But in the end, you really just have a few more guns to clean.

The other thing the great leaders like Tom Buning give are the standards by which a soldier is measured. Men like him tell us what is expected, and it is our responsibility to exceed those standards.

And while many Americans all too often don't set standards for themselves nor concern themselves with striving to meet standards set by others, soldiers go above and beyond whatever expectations and standards are set. They don't want to say, "We passed with high grades"; instead, we want to crush what is considered excellent.

The mission and standards come from our leaders. But it is our job to adapt in the field when things don't go as well as planned.

We trust leaders to give us our mission and set the standards, and in return, they trust us to adapt and excel. Imagine how great America would be if everyone worked this way.

CHAPTER 8

TONY BANDIERA
Vietnam

INTRODUCTION:

When I moved to Dallas, Texas, lots of Special Forces guys connected with me, especially the older ones. They knew that as a new civilian, I'd be trying to find my place in life. That's why a mutual friend introduced me to Tony Bandiera.

Tony was a Green Beret in Vietnam. It was a different time back then. Soldiers weren't presented with American flags and cheers when they came home. They were spit on and called murderers and baby killers after sacrificing to keep this country free. I can't imagine coming back to my country with that treatment.

Tony chose not only to serve in the military but to take it to the highest levels in the Special Forces. That alone impressed me when I met him—to think, here is a guy who is going to make the best of the situation, no matter what people think.

After the war, he became a businessman. He decided to go after it and make the American dream happen. He worked himself up to owning a very successful business where he now thrives as CEO and president.

Tony listened to his mentors when he got out of the service. He has one mentor in particular whom he credits with making him the man he is today. And Tony is paying that gift forward by mentoring me. I can tell you there is nothing more empowering than having a man like Tony as a mentor.

Over the years, Tony has started many businesses with a no-quit attitude. And like every man in this book, he is humble. He doesn't promote what he does now or what he did overseas. He is a quiet, charismatic person who continues his mission to be a good steward of this country.

Soldiers are soldiers first; they will always answer the call. When I gave Tony a call about the Legacy Jump, there wasn't any hesitation. "Just let me know where to be," he said.

VIETNAM:

I never wanted to go into the military. My father and uncle both served. I thought that was cool, but people were dying in Vietnam. I had no desire to put my life on the line.

Then I got a draft notice, so I moved from Tulsa, Oklahoma, to Texas to avoid the notice. But then I got another notice, so I moved back to Tulsa.

My father sat me down and said, "Son, you can't keep doing this. You're going to have to make a decision. You need to figure out what you want and do the right thing."

I decided if I was going in, I would have a better chance of picking a meaningful job if I enlisted. I contacted my cousin Sam Woods and our high school buddy Hud Huddleston.

We would enlist under the "Buddy Plan." Our understanding was that we would serve our three years together; however, fate had other plans for me. We were separated after Basic Training. I was sent to AIT (Advance Individual Training) at Fort Leonard Wood, Missouri. Then I volunteered for Jump School at Fort Benning, Georgia. After Jump School, I was assigned to the 82nd Airborne Division stationed at Fort Bragg, North Carolina.

After a short stint there, I received orders to join the 101st Airborne Division in Vietnam. I was truly excited about being assigned to the "Screaming Eagles." But fate jumped up again and bit me on the ass.

As we were being processed in at Camp Alpha in Cam Ranh Bay, the whole lot of us were rerouted to the 1st Brigade of the 1st Cavalry. Prior to our arrival, elements of the 1st Cavalry had been in contact with the enemy and sustained a large number of casualties. Fortunately for me, I was assigned to the S-2 (Intelligence Section) of an engineer battalion. After six months in this position, Captain Cook (my CO) and I were assigned temporary duty to a Special Forces A camp at Bảng Sản.

I wasn't prepared, but pleasantly surprised at the incredible wealth of knowledge and professionalism that emanated from these Green Berets. I was treated as a person, not a serial number.

During my stay, I was invited to go on night patrols as well as participate in reconnaissance of the local area. I knew I was out of my element, but they brought me along. Needless to say, I soaked up as much as I could and cherished every minute of my three months at Bảng Sản. All good things must come to an end, so I returned to my unit.

I wondered,"Do I have what it takes to make it through the John F. Kennedy School for Special Warfare?"

At the end of my enlistment, a recruiter asked me to consider reenlisting and being assigned to whatever unit I wanted. I told him my decision to stay would be predicated on serving with the best of the best—Special Forces. So I was accepted in the next class.

The light and heavy weapons course was intense. I had to learn how to use all the American weapons systems as well as those of our enemy. I also learned to plan and execute camp defense from different camp designs, such as triangular, rectangular, and star shapes.

I learned quickly that Special Forces is like having a bunch of alpha dogs in a kennel, with one exception: In Special Forces, there is a time to lead and a time to follow. Teamwork is the core of brotherhood. This was the catalyst that changed my life.

Once in Vietnam, the group was broken down. Some went to the A-Camps along the Laotian and Cambodian border. The rest, about 10 to 15 percent of us, were assigned to MACVSOG (Military Assistance Command Vietnam Studies and Observation Group).

At the time, this unit was the most classified unit in Vietnam. The mention of the name to unauthorized personnel could get you in deep trouble.

MACVSOG had a few locations. The one I was assigned to was called CCN (Command and Control North) in Da Nang. Our primary function was to gather information on the enemy in denied areas like Laos and Cambodia.

Our reconnaissance teams were comprised of Vietnamese, Chinese Nungs, Montagnards (various tribes, but mostly Bru), and former North Vietnamese Army soldiers. I was assigned to RT-Asp commanded by SFC Larry Trimble. Through his leadership, we developed a bond that is hard to put into words, but it was felt. The thought of losing any of my brothers in combat was too painful to comprehend. The welfare of the team was my main focus.

As a team, we were mission oriented. Needless to say, we sometimes had a difference of opinion, but the mission kept us tight and opinions never got in the way.

SFC Trimble became a Covey Rider (a seasoned recon team leader who rides in a Forward Air Controller aircraft), and I became One-Zero or team leader. I got two men, sergeants Phil Quinn and Gene Pugh, both with combat experience.

I remember one impactful mission. We launched out of NKP (Nakhon Phanom Royal Thai Air Force Base in Thailand). We were going in heavy with 10 men, so we split the team. Sgt. Pugh rode with me and half the team, and the rest were in the other helicopter with Sgt. Quinn.

Because of the distance we needed to travel, we refueled at a secret-agency-controlled location. Our communication relay site was Leg Horn, another classified site. And to complicate matters further, we had piggyback targets.

As we approached the primary landing zone (LZ), we were shocked because it was covered with stumps that were not revealed in the surveillance photographs.

Covey stated that he could see enemy movement near the LZ, so I aborted the primary LZ insertion and headed toward the secondary LZ.

When we got to the second LZ, we discovered that it was covered with tall grass. While we looked for a place to land, we started receiving ground fire. I told the pilots to abort and to advise Covey of the situation.

As our helicopter was banking away, I noticed that the helicopter carrying Sgt. Quinn had landed. I told the pilot not to move away because my team was in trouble. Sgt. Quinn was on the ground without a radio. I had to get to him fast.

I tapped the pilot on the head with my rifle, motioning for him to land. He didn't. So I yelled at Sgt. Pugh to stay with the team, and I jumped the eight to 10 feet to the grassy slope. I knew the grass was long, but I was surprised to discover that it was armpit high.

I landed at a downward angle, and my ankle buckled, causing me to pitch forward. My head hit the only rock on the LZ, knocking me out.

I wasn't out for long, but when I opened my eyes, I was

starring into our interpreter's face. Next to him was Sgt. Pugh. They had seen me go down hard and they did what brothers do. When Pugh saw me sprawled helplessly on the ground, he jumped after me.

As they hoisted me back into the helicopter, Covey directed cover from A-1As and A-1Es out of Thailand.

Sgt. Pugh immediately tended to my ankle. He stabilized my foot and kept me abreast of what was happening at the LZ. I was disappointed in myself for getting injured and down on myself for not being in the fight.

After the long flight back, they tended to me in the hospital. Phil Quinn came to see me and personally thank me for saving him and the other team members. I was proud of his words.

When he departed, he said, "See you soon, brother." Little did I know that was the last time I would ever see Phil.

I also discovered that Gene Pugh had sprained his ankle when he had leaped to save me.

As a Special Forces soldier, I understood that completing the mission was the number one priority. I continue that attitude in civilian life. When I was discharged, I was shocked by the number of civilians who would settle for mediocrity.

I am proud to be part of the Special Forces legacy. I was extremely fortunate to have served with a group of elite soldiers who share my core values.

Those values have driven me in business. The dedication to mission and team have given me an edge. I have a solid team, and we are dedicated to each other in the pursuit of our mission. That is the key to my success.

In war, teammates are trusted brothers, but brotherhood extends far beyond combat. Soldiers make lifelong friends who often carry over into civilian life. I personally have met young soldiers after their military service, and there is an instant brotherhood connection.

After my discharge, I lost contact with Gene Pugh and my other teammates. But as luck would have it, in the mid-1980s, I received an early morning phone call.

The caller asked, "Is this Tony Bandiera?"

"Yes, it is. Who's this?"

"How's your ankle? You broke it on March 8, 1969."

"No one knows about..." I replied.

"Tony, it's me, Gene."

At the beginning, I didn't recognize his voice. Then it hit me. I was instantly filled with emotions from the past. I felt like a fresh breeze blew through me. A brother, a life-and-death experience brother, was on the phone. I fought side by side with him. He came to my aid, just like I would have come to his.

"I never had a chance to thank you," I said.

"Then buy me a beer."

That's the soldier's currency—a simple beer.

Once we reconnected, he got me involved in Chapter XXXI of the Special Forces Association. I met the members and felt like I found my family of brothers again.

Eventually Gene came to work for me. I knew his loyalty level and that he could be trusted. He is a true brother.

BIRDMAN:

Every man in this book speaks about brotherhood. As Special Forces veterans, Tony and I had a different perspective on brotherhood because our teams were smaller and our units were tightly knit. But every soldier has his day.

Fighting side by side with your team, watching the back of the man on your left and on your right is an experience each of the men in this book recognizes. The difference for Tony and me was our training and how incredibly dependent we were on our teams.

When I finally joined up with my platoon, I knew to keep my mouth shut, to do my time, and earn their respect. You have to prove that you can save their lives and watch their backs in war before they accept you. The platoon will welcome you in at some point if you do your job and exceed expectations.

When I got to my platoon, I was told I had to get the SEAL trident sewn onto my cammies. I went to the store and they gave me a 1980s version of the trident. But since I was brand new, I didn't know the difference.

I showed up at the platoon, proud to be a member of the exclusive group, and the guys were like "What the hell is that? Oh, you think you're a Frogman?" They weren't being mean, just poking fun at the new guy.

I thought, "Damn it. I screwed up right off the bat." Now the pressure was on to prove myself.

When you're new to a team, you're assigned a primary. A primary is a teammate who is in charge of a department you're in. My primary was a sniper. He expected nothing less than perfection. He didn't have time to watch me all day. He would push, push, push and expect, expect, expect. I tried really hard to go above and beyond, but it never seemed like I was good enough.

One day we were on the shooting range. After we took our shots, we walked out to the targets. I looked at mine; I'd dialed it in really well, shooting in a small group. I was pretty proud of the grouping.

My primary looked over my shoulder, "Not bad," he said. "Not bad."

He casually let me look at his target. I was shocked. He had sent every bullet through the same hole. I was like, "You got to be kidding me!"

The Team in Iraq

"I won," he said. "Buy me a case of beer."

He had beat me, and I was the new guy, so I bought him the beer.

When we were drinking, he told me he had been shooting off target the whole time. Then, when we picked up our targets, he punched a hole in his.

So I had actually won. But I hadn't been paying attention, and for that reason, he had won. I don't know whether he was teaching me to pay attention to my surroundings or if he just wanted to screw with me. Either way, he won.

That day, my teammate let me know that winning isn't always about doing the obvious. Sometimes, we need to think outside the box to move past the competition, or in war, outsmart our enemy.

In Alpha Platoon, we call ourselves the Bad Karma Platoon. We had a killer patch, and I wanted it so badly. So I asked my primary, "Dude, how do I get one of those?"

"You have to earn it, man," he said over his shoulder as he walked away from me.

It turned out that that patch is harder to get than the SEAL Trident because it's not just about passing or failing evolutions; you have to earn the trust of your team. Until they feel comfortable with you, there's no way you get that damn thing. You just keep doing your job, and it will come when it comes, hopefully!

We were getting into the final phase of training, and I was cleaning targets with some other guys when I saw my primary walking purposefully toward us. I thought, "Oh boy. What's going to happen here?"

He walked straight up to me and said, "We all had a

vote." He took out a patch and put it on my chest. "You earned it, brother."

It blew me away. This was the guy who rode me hard. I was never good enough. My best was never good enough for him. When I thought I succeeded, he'd shrug and point out where I hadn't been perfect.

And now he was the one to give me my patch. I was so fired up, so proud. I wore that patch for every operation overseas, and when I came back, I had it framed. It's on the wall of my office today to remind me of brotherhood and the importance of working with your team.

But just getting the patch wasn't enough. I had to continue to prove that I was worthy of owning it and wearing it. Each member was accountable to the group and each person on the team. Our responsibility is not to look out for ourselves, but for our brothers. The team only works when each of us is looking after the man on our right and left and not worrying about ourselves because we know that our brothers are looking after us just as intently. Our lives are in their hands, just like theirs are in ours.

Each teammate in the platoon has a different role. No one is more important than anyone else because each role is vital to our success. Maybe one role gets more attention or one member gets more recognition, but we know that our success is based on the hard work of each member of the team. The only reason we come home alive at the end of the day is because our brothers go above and beyond for us.

Yes, as well-trained soldiers, we are proud of our abilities. There is some internal confidence, cockiness even. But this comes from knowing that our abilities contribute to the team's success. We will be able to complete our mission because each one of us excels to the highest level.

If I'm on a shooting range and my buddy shoots better than me that day, he is laughing at me. I'm not having that. We are doing it again. Load it up, and this time I better beat him. And we have to do it as many times as it takes for me to beat him. It doesn't make me a better person than him, but we are always challenging each other toward perfection.

The first time you go out on target overseas and you must count on your team to cover down on the area, you realize how important each teammate is. You rely on them, and they rely on you. You can trust their skills and abilities because together you perfected them. And that is how brotherhood is created.

SEAL training taught me to say, "I don't know if I can make it, but what I don't know doesn't mean I can't."

CHAPTER 9

RICHARD "DICK" AGNEW
Korea

INTRODUCTION:

Good old Richard Agnew! "Ryan, call me Dick," he'd say.

Dick is one hell of a character; 80-some years old and still getting after it.

He was a paratrooper during the Korean War and received the Distinguished Service Cross for his commitment to his fellow teammates. If you ask him about receiving the medal, he won't tell you about what happened. He says, "The incident that happened that day is always in the back of my head. Always. I try to forget about it, but it never goes away. So why talk about it?"

Everything Dick does is squared away. His military

boots are still shined and ready to go. He doesn't have a cell phone. He doesn't have an e-mail address. He does everything by mail, landline phone calls, and face-to-face meetings. If you don't agree with him or you don't meet up to his expectations, he will let you know. He doesn't require much, and he always wants to help.

When I was looking for a jumper for the Korean War, a mentor of mine, Steve Woods, mentioned Dick. We spent a good month tracking him down because he's still on the go, even in his 80s.

I was nervous because we were running out of time before the jump. When we finally had a phone number, I called Dick and said, "Sir, this is Ryan. You don't know who I am, but I spent eight years in the service, the majority of that time as a SEAL. We've got this pretty cool event going on. We are about to do a skydive with one jumper from every war from WWII to the present day. We are looking for someone to represent Korea."

He goes "Really? When?" There wasn't even a second thought about it.

I gave him some details and he asked, "Can we jump solo or do we have to do that hooked-up-to-a-buddy crap?"

I said, "Sir, unfortunately, if you aren't qualified to sky-dive..."

He interrupted me, "I'm in."

I said, "Wow! It's an honor."

Dick has been waiting since the 1950s to jump again. He was ready to answer the call.

He's still a soldier at heart and continues to serve his country. He's done all kinds of fundraising to help promote America, and he's sat on many boards. If there's something that needs to be done, he will take care of it himself. He doesn't wait for anyone else. He is one of my strongest mentors. He teaches me about being professional in every-thing I do.

KOREA:

I joined the Army when I was 16. Life was tough for my family at the time. When I was 14, my family moved into a boarding house after we were evicted from our home. When my mother procured a job at a children's home in Cromwell, Connecticut, she could only take one child with her, and the one child was my sister Gloria. My brother went to Wyoming, and I joined the Army Airborne.

Coming from those conditions, the barracks weren't so bad. We had two squads living upstairs and two squads downstairs. The latrine had no doors on the stalls and no lids on the toilets. There were four toilets and six sinks for all of the soldiers to use. This meant that we had to shave and take care of our personal hygiene and sanitary needs in a matter of minutes. Of course, I was so young that I wasn't shaving yet, so that gave me an extra minute each day.

From day one in the Army, we were building a team. Togetherness is very important in the armed forces. You get to know the intimacies, the likes, dislikes, the disappointments, and achievements of your brothers. That is very important because you are creating a team. Ultimately, when decisions need to be made, everyone knows pretty much the strong points and weaknesses of each other.

We were a band of brothers. I shared things with my brothers, and they would in turn share things with me. Sometimes they would say, "Hey, Aggie. What do you think about such and such? I want to know what you think." And I'd ask their opinions because I wanted to know their viewpoints before giving mine. This back and forth created togetherness and unity. In the process, you develop that strong camaraderie.

I didn't have much civilian attire back then. I think I had two civilian shirts, one long sleeve for the winter and one short sleeve. I had one pair of trousers. I also had one pair of civilian shoes and one pair of civilian socks. Everything else I wore was issued by the Army.

Back then, none of the soldiers had his own car. We didn't need them. If we were in uniform, we could hitch-hike into town. Someone was sure to see us, pick us up, and take us to our destination.

I used to hitchhike from Fort Bragg, North Carolina, to Boston, Massachusetts, to see my family and then hitch-hike back. People would pick me up and drive me for miles. I've had families give me a $20 bill and send me to a res-taurant to get drinks, burgers, and fries. One family even let me drive their car to go get food. Others would pay for my motel accommodations.

Do you think people would do that for a GI today?

One time, my assistant squad leader and I hitchhiked to his family's home in Hickory, North Carolina. The family was very cordial and nice to me.

His father asked me if I wanted a drink. I said, "A drink of what?"

He said, "I make my own," and left the room.

I didn't know what he was talking about. I thought may-be he made his own soda or lemonade.

His son, the corporal, said, "Hey, Dick, my dad makes moonshine. If you said yes to a drink, he's getting you some moonshine. Whatever you do, sip it."

Well, moonshine didn't mean anything me. I was just a kid.

His father returned with a small glass half full. The corporal warned again, "Sip it. Take your time. Just wet your tongue."

I followed his instructions and slowly drank the hooch. I felt pretty good, until I stood up. The room started spinning and getting a bit hazy. So I sat back down.

His dad asked, "What do you think, Dick? Pretty smooth?"

"Yes." I didn't want to insult the father and tell him it was the worse thing I'd ever tasted.

"Would you like another one, Dick?"

Again, I wanted to be polite. And I didn't want to insult him, so I said, "Yes."

My friend was out of the room at the time. Had he been there, I'm sure he would have stopped me when his father made the offer.

After the second drink, when I stood up, I passed out.

I woke up the next morning with my shirt and trousers off, socks and boots off, in just skivvies and a T-shirt. I'd been undressed where I had fallen. That was my introduction to moonshine.

In the military in my time, you did what they told you. You didn't ask questions. I knew sergeants who had a third-grade education. Some could barely read. But they knew the Army, and they knew how to take care of us and how to keep us alive.

I will never forget one sergeant, a big, burly fellow. He always called me Shithead. Whatever we were doing, he'd say, "Isn't that right, Shithead?" Or "When are you going to learn, Shithead?" Or worse, "Give me 60 push-ups, Shithead." After I did them, he'd say, "I didn't like those. Give me 20 more, Shithead." And he'd keep doing this until I'd done 60 to 100 push-ups.

During the seventh week of training, we boarded a C-47 (Skytrain). It was the first time I'd been up in an airplane. I was scared to death. I remember looking out the window and seeing the wings fluttering like they were going to fall off.

Because my last name began with an A, I was closest to the door. That old sergeant was actually hanging out of the door. At 900 feet, he signaled us and the red light went on. We stood up.

He commanded us to check our equipment and hook the handles of our parachutes to the anchor lines on the plane.

Then he had us sound off. The guy whose name was closest to Z started, and they counted all the way down.

"Eight, okay."

"Seven, okay."

"Six, okay."

Until they got to me. "One, okay."

Then the red light turned to green. We were above 1,000 feet. The sergeant motioned me forward. "Okay, Private Agnew."

I didn't know who he was talking to. It was the first time he'd used my real name. It had been so long since I'd heard my name, I didn't recognize it.

"Let's go, son." He was so nice, cordial, and brotherly.

He reminded me how to stand at the door with one

foot outside on the platform. I remember thinking, "He's human after all."

Then he said, "Don't look at the ground."

Of course I did. That made things worse.

"Look at the big cloud out there," he pointed. "When I tap you on the butt, out you go."

A good leader knows how to cultivate his troops in such a way that they know what the leader knows. If you don't know, you're in trouble, and your team is in trouble. When the team knows what the leader knows, they will then respect the leader for passing the knowledge along. And they, in turn, will pass it along to someone else. This builds a strong team.

The mission is the number one priority. I have always felt that an aggressively executed profile or mannerism is about getting your people involved, sharing with them what needs to be done, challenging them, and then supporting them during crunch time.

Leadership is not saying, "I want you to do this. I want you to do that." When you say "I, I, I" or "you, you, you," as in "You need to..." and "You did...," you are building up a defense mechanism.

If you say "we" instead, they will join you. You become part of a team. Say, "We need to accomplish this."

Tell them what needs to be done and your ideas about how to accomplish it. And let them be part of the solution and accomplishment. If a leader says something and the people on the team don't raise their hands when they disagree, the leader hasn't gotten through. Many times, people sitting in front of you might have a far better insight than yours.

Say, "Now, I want feedback. How can we do it better?" People want to be part of the team. And they want to have a purpose. And when they do, they'll lay down their lives for the team.

What's more important is giving credit when the mission is complete. You can say, "Hey, look what we've done." Not I, not me, but we. People need to be recognized.

In the military, leadership can be a life or death thing. Civilian life isn't the same, but the mission is still important. Leaders need to know what their subordinates can or can't do. They need to train their people toward their advantage.

Over the years and generations, the military is the same in a lot of ways, and in some ways it isn't. Uniforms change. Tactics change. Weapons change. Ammunition changes. But the soldier and mission is always the same. It is always constant. Your objective might change, but not the mission. The mission is the same.

BIRDMAN:

L eaders inspire us. They motivate us. And they know what it takes to get us to where we need to go. In military training, there is a lot of ribbing, yelling, and quite a bit of payment for your mistakes. This is so we won't be arrogant and self-absorbed. They are training us to set ourselves aside so we can focus on the mission and the team.

Like Dick's sergeant, I've had a few leaders yell at me and give me crap, but once I passed, they were there to support me so I could be a better teammate.

In training, when we screwed up, the instructors made us do crazy things to drill in the lesson. For instance, one day I was forced to do a tire pull. This is where you pull a big old tractor tire from one house to the next and back. The tire is huge and heavy, and it's exhausting to pull it. It may seem like a silly punishment, but it does cause you to pay attention to the techniques and tactics they're teaching you; plus, you're raising your resting heart rate to simulate the stresses of war.

At first, you feel the instructors are just being assholes, but later you realize that it is all part of the plan.

Of course, when you are part of the team, your leaders treat you differently. Some are still cocky, but most treat you with respect.

For instance, our platoon had this thing called a roundtable. This was where everyone drops rank and has a man-to-man conversation. We then get everything off our chests, settle it as men, move on, and get back to work.

My command master chief used to come in the room and kick all the officers out. He'd say, "I need some time with the E-dogs." He was old school and really cool. He had a commanding presence, six foot three inches, and a bald head. He'd look at everybody and ask, "How's morale?"

Being a new guy, I was afraid to speak up. But one time he asked, "How's morale?" and looked at me and then my name tag. He said, "Hey, Parrott, how's morale?"

I was like, "I'm just happy to be here."

He said, "That's bullshit. How's morale?"

I said, "Well, we could use more weapons in the armory."

He said, "All right. Parrott needs weapons. What else have you got?" And he looked at the other guys.

When we were done, he went to the commanding officer and requested what we'd asked for and got us squared away.

Being a leader involves knowing what's truly important to the team and sticking your neck out there to ensure the troops have the correct tools. At the end of the day, the true leader will say, "The only reason I'm sitting at the top today is because all of you guys are holding me up."

In the military, your team is also your leader. The old-timers teach the new guys. At times, your peers give you an ass-chewing. Most of the time, they're trying to teach you lessons. But admittedly, sometimes they just feel like giving you a tough time.

In the military, ball-busting creates camaraderie. Lessons are taught and new people are put in their places. As we go through these experiences together, either as the newbie or as part of the group in on the joke, we develop our sense of a team.

For instance, on my first deployment, the one that

ended with me getting blown out of our Humvee, our mission was to look for a weapons cache site on an island.

Since I was the new guy, I got to do all the shit-work. They gave me first watch, and I was amped up.

That was when they told me about this mythical cat on the island. The other guys told me about how crazy the cat was. Maybe it was a leopard. Maybe it was a big-ass mountain lion. The previous teams saw it, but they couldn't get a bead on it. It may have attacked some locals.

I was wigging out, saying "Serious, dude?"

"Yes," they all agreed.

They had me stand about five feet away from our site to make sure the cat didn't get too close.

Of course they were messing with me. But being new, I believed them.

When the day rolled in and there was no cat to be found, I finally got the idea that they were bullshitting me. I watched as they began smiling and then laughing at me. At first I was embarrassed, but then I was laughing with them. In a weird way, I felt closer to the team after spending the night protecting them from a nonexistent cat.

I learned the importance of being diligent on watch, even when it doesn't seem like there is a serious threat out there. SEALs are always training, even in their down time, even when they are busting each other's balls. New guys need to learn quickly before heading into war. Old-timers have learned certain things that you can't learn in BUD/S or other formal training.

That's why you're treated like a dog when you're new. As a new guy, expect it. But when we're deployed, things change. The toughness instilled by the team guys plays an

Blurry shots of me the morning after standing watch for the big mythical cat

important role; plus, from a training perspective, each of us needs to know what the others know. New people must learn from the mistakes of the old-timers. They need every tool possible to be successful. And it is the more senior leader's responsibility to share and train the new guy.

When we are focused on mission and team, there is no holding back. When we rely on others for our very survival, we want to make sure they are in the best shape possible, that they know everything we know and everything they need to know to complete the mission.

I wonder...if businesses had this type of accountability and understanding, whether more could get accomplished. People wouldn't horde information, and they wouldn't be threatened when someone on the team is more enthusiastic and energetic because that would mean that we would all succeed. Perhaps it can begin with a dedication to each other and the team.

CHAPTER 10

PETER BIELSKIS
World War II

INTRODUCTION:

When it came to arranging jumpers for the Legacy Jump, you can imagine that finding someone to represent World War II was difficult. Every time we found WWII vets, they might be willing, but their health or other circumstances kept them from joining us. These guys are in their 80s and 90s. Their minds tell them they can jump, but their bodies are saying, "Hell, no."

We thought we had a gentleman, but then he canceled with weeks to go. I searched the Internet, looking up every WWII veteran who was still alive and called him. As stressful as it was, the cool thing was hearing all their inspiring stories. I heard stories about invading the beaches of Normandy, jumping out of planes over Europe, and fighting in the Pacific. These iconic WWII veterans are dying off at hundreds per day, and we're losing their stories. And I had the opportunity to hear many of them.

After about 30 or so phone calls, I thought, "There's got to be a better way."

I called a buddy from Michigan named Gary Tanner, who was also the Veteran of the Year. I filled him in on what we needed, and he said, "Give me an hour."

Within one hour's time, he had a gentleman named Peter Bielskis. Once I had a phone number, I called Peter.

He answered with one of those raspy, old-school voices.

I said, "Sir, I heard you want to jump out of a plane."

He said, "Oh, yeah."

"What do you think about jumping out of a perfectly good World War II plane?"

He laughed and said, "Ryan, I served in World War II. I was a B17 ball turret gunner, and I never once in 27 combat missions had to jump out of an airplane."

During that time in the war, there was a high attrition rate for airmen. But Peter made it through. He says he didn't do much during the war, but he did. Because of the high attrition rate, he and his team developed new strategies and tactics. Their ideas made us the soldiers we are today. Yet Peter is more than humble. You can't get many words out of him, no matter how hard you try.

When I asked him if he wanted to join us for the jump, he didn't say yes or no; instead, he said, "Whatever you think."

"Sir, I'm not clear," I responded.

He said, "Of course."

I couldn't believe my ears. Here's a guy who is 88 years

old and had never jumped from a plane in his life, and now he wants to answer the call to help our veterans. That is the coolest thing in the world.

We literally had two weeks until the jump. We had to include him in the promotion and get him a jump suit. We had no time to do the normal prep.

Peter flew from Michigan to Texas at 88 years old to jump out of a plane for the first time in his life. Talk about commitment! That man will never stop serving his country.

When we were about to get into the plane, I could tell that he was nervous. I asked him if he was ready.

He said, "Well, if I could find a getaway car right now, I might just take it."

Peter is one of the most iconic men I've ever met. He's jumped twice now. He said he may retire when he's 90. But then again, he's waiting for the call.

WORLD WAR II:

It was a long time ago. I joined the Air Force in 1944 and then went overseas in 1945. I knew that someone had to fight for my country. I was physically fit, and my country needed help. I don't know how else to describe it.

I flew with the 8th Air Force for 27 missions. From that relatively short experience, I learned a lesson that stayed with me the rest of my life: You have to depend on the buddy with you. And he depends on you.

I learned about dedication to my country, the mission, and buddies from my father. He fought in World War I. He came to America from Lithuania in 1912 and joined the Army a few years later. He said, "This is my country now. Somebody's got to protect it." He wasn't even a citizen then, but he was committed to the United States.

I remember him saying, "I came to this country and they shipped me back to Europe. At least I didn't have to pay for it that time." He was looking for freedom for himself and his family, and he was willing to fight for it. It was good enough for him; it was good enough for me.

Back in World War II, things were different, both in how we fought and in the equipment we had. For instance, the plane I flew in had a crew of 10. I was in the ball turret under the plane. We'd fly in these massive formations, and I was hanging down below the plane shooting my machine gun at any target that appeared.

I tried to get into pilot training, but I didn't qualify because I didn't have enough education. All of the pilots were college students and I was just out of high school. Two of us were about the same height and weight. The other guy went to the tail gun, so I went in the ball underneath the plane. I have no idea why they picked me for the turret. Maybe I was too dumb for anything else, so they said put him in the turret and see what he can do. I'm also sure it had to do with my size. They put the smallest guys in the turret.

The only good thing about it is when you are flying, you see everything below and around you. You're surrounded by glass. Anything coming up from the bottom is what I was shooting.

If something ever went wrong, I had to depend on the other men to get me out of the turret. If there was no mechanical problem, I could get in or out myself. If there was a problem, then they had to crank me out. I was dependent on them.

I also didn't have a parachute inside. If something happened, there might not be enough time to get a parachute and put it on. And back then, planes were always getting shot out of the sky. I've thought about that a lot since those days, but when you're young, you don't think.

The whole time I was there, we only lost one airplane in the squadron. Four of the 10 people on the plane ejected. The rest were killed. The sobering thing for me is that they were the first crew I flew with.

When we were flying, we would see all the flack around us. But at the end of mission, we came back to a nice bunk and hot meal. Then we wouldn't do anything until the next mission. It could be tomorrow or three or four days because of the weather. But we always had nice food, a good bed to sleep in, and good company.

You got to know your crew. They were your family. You flew with them, you slept with them, and you had to depend on them to bring you back.

This is the foundation that you have in the service. It's the most terrific thing. No matter what, you have to support your fellows. I feel that so many people have forgotten this. It boils down to who is with you, your buddies.

Teamwork is everything, regardless of where you are. Even in civilian life, if you can get along with someone else, it makes things a lot easier. A lot of people are just for "me." They only look out for themselves. They are going to be a sorry bunch of people.

The biggest mission we did involved probably 1,200 airplanes, including bombers and fighters. It was just one stream after another. Right now you've got an airplane that sits back about a mile and it shoots off a missile. But when you have over 1,000 airplanes in the air, it's something you'll never see again. I don't know how they kept from colliding with each other.

My pilot was a hotshot. When they closed up formation, he almost touched the other airplanes. He was a terrific pilot, but sometimes you don't want to get that close, like when you take off with a bomb load so heavy; you barely clear the trees at the end of the airfield. Sometimes we'd scrape some of the trees on the bottom of our airplane. Fortunately, I wasn't inside the turret until we were at 10,000 or 12,000 feet and in enemy territory.

Sometimes I would stay in the turret for up to three hours, sometimes four, depending on where we were going. The worst part about it is if you had to go to the bathroom, you were in trouble. Of course the length of the missions was much longer, sometimes up to eight hours. I didn't go into the turret until we encountered fighter planes.

I had a job to do and that was it. I can't really say anything else. When you are young, you don't think much about it. I was nervous. I used to get sick before the mission. But that didn't stop me. My country and my crew were depending on me.

During my 27 missions in the 8th Air Force, I never had to jump out of an airplane. When I turned 88, the Sons of the Flag got me to jump out of a plane for the first time.

As far as I know, I'm the last one still alive from our crew. The last man who I was in contact with was our radio operator, and he passed away Christmas two years ago. While our generation is moving on, I'm glad that the values and traditions that were taught to me continue to be taught to young people in the service today. Through us, the tradition continues.

BIRDMAN:

In the military, we respect tradition. We know that we stand in a long line of service men and women, stretching all the way back to the founding of our nation. We value those who have gone before us; we acknowledge their contribution and know that we are able to fight for freedom because they paved the way back then.

In exchange for their contribution, we continue the traditions that they started and pass along the values they developed.

In my case, I've always had a soft spot for the World War II soldiers because both my grandfathers served. They were real men. Listening to their stories growing up made me who I am today.

I was proud to be able to introduce my grandfathers to some of my team members when I was in sniper school. One weekend, I said, "Hey, let's get out of here. Let's visit my family in Michigan." We were in Indiana, so it was a four-hour drive, and we only got Sundays off. So the minute we were done on Saturday, we were in the car.

We made it just in time to eat at my Aunt Tweet and Uncle Gary's steakhouse. My whole family was there to greet us. It was the chance for both of my grandfathers to meet my teammates. I watched my grandfathers' faces as they shook hands with these modern warriors. I could see that it re-ignited the fire they had when they were young soldiers. They began telling stories and laughing with us. It meant a lot to me that these seven guys from different platoons and SEAL teams visited my family during their time off. Then again, who doesn't want a free steak?

Group of guys from sniper school meeting with my family and grandfathers, who both served in World War II

First Sergeant Caston "Buck" Parrott, United States Army, World War II

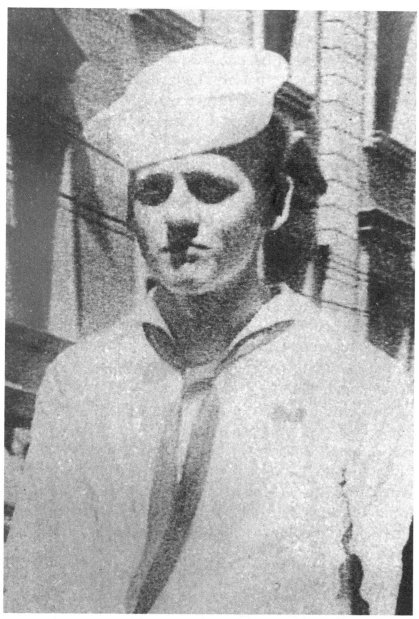

Gunner's Mate, Third Class Petty Officer Richard "Dutch" Hayner, United States Navy, World War II

The day I lost one of my grandfathers was a pivotal time in my life as a soldier.

We'd just gotten back to base at the conclusion of an operation. I noticed that my chief was talking to the task unit commander. These were great guys. They were always there to greet us at the end of a mission. But on this day, there was a weird context to our return; instead of greeting us, they were talking with each other. I knew nothing went off course on this operation, so what could this be?

Finally, my chief walked toward us. The whole platoon was still awaiting word from him. He walked directly to me and stopped, "Hey, man, I just want to be the one to tell you this because I knew him too. Your granddaddy has passed away."

That news was really difficult for me because I loved both my grandfathers. To hear this news following back-to-back operations was terrible.

I looked at my chief and asked, "Which one?" because he had met both of my grandfathers.

"Caston."

All I could say was, "Damn."

Grandpa "Buckaroo," my father's father, lived the fullest life. But he was also a stubborn SOB. Before World War II, he was a Tennessee farmer. When he returned from war, he became a firefighter in Detroit for 30 years. He was an honorable man who put the flag outside his house every day.

But in the last few years, he had gone blind, needed a walker, and had been developing dementia.

My senior chief and commander joined me while I processed the news. One of them gave me a satellite phone to call my dad.

When he answered, I said, "Hey, Pop." He knew why I was calling. I'm sure he felt even worse than I did, so I didn't waste any time. "What can I do? Do you want me to come home?"

It was the first time in my life my dad was speechless. Finally he said, "I don't know how to answer that."

I had already made up my mind that if I got clearance, had no mission in the next few days, and could find a plane, I'd go home.

After the call, my chief asked, "What do you want to do, brother?"

I waved my hand in the air in a circle, which means

Support of the Brotherhood

"Let's rally up and get it going."

My task unit commander rushed to make sure that Communications was open and we were ready to go. My chief grabbed my information to look for plane flights for me. Typically, we fly birds in and out, but they only come once a month. My commander was able to find a plane heading out the next day that could get me to an airport. From there, I could go standby to get back to Detroit.

I packed a bag for a one- or two-day trip. I didn't have my military uniform, just my dress cammies, and they still had the salt, sweat, and the smell of Iraq on them. But they were professional-looking enough.

When I touched down in Detroit, I went straight to the funeral home. It was early in the morning and I was the first to show up.

When the funeral home people answered the door, I said, "I would like to see Caston Parrott."

They said he wasn't ready for viewing.

I said, "I want to see him."

"But only immediate family can see him."

I was standing there in my tan desert cammies. I said, "Well, look on the name tag of my uniform. Obviously, I'm family."

"We're sorry, only immediate family."

I got really pissed off because here I am 48 hours after being in combat and my grandfather is lying there in a casket, and they won't afford me the respect to pay him homage for his service and sacrifice for this country. He was probably just 20 feet from me in another room. I said, "Whoever the funeral home director is, I want to talk to that person right now."

When he came in, I said, "Do you see what's on my

name tag? I don't think you can get any closer to immediate family than that. My grandfather served in the War. And I'm the only other member on this side of the family to serve. Get me to see my grandfather so I can salute him and send him home. Then I can be strong when my family arrives."

Finally, they opened the doors. I had seen enough dead bodies in my life that it didn't matter if the body was ready for viewing. I just wanted to talk to Gramps, to get my peace.

> *"Live for something rather than die for nothing."*
> —George Patton

I stood there looking at him in the casket, remembering all the fun times we'd had and all the cool stuff he had shared with me about the military. He didn't talk with anyone else in the family like he did with me.

I remembered back to our prior Christmas. He was 93 and had dementia. He couldn't remember new stuff, but he always remembered the old stuff. He could remember names and ranks in the military.

Our family was at his house, and even though his macular degeneration and glaucoma had made him as blind as a bat, he knew he had a picture of an old-school fire engine on his wall, and he knew exactly where it was. He couldn't see it, but he pointed to it and said, "Hey, you know that picture right there? I want you to have it." He knew how much I'd idolized him for being a firefighter as well as a military soldier.

I said, "Gramps, if I get that picture, then I want you to autograph it for me."

It took him about 20 practice tries on a piece of paper

to figure out his signature. He couldn't see what he was writing; plus, he hadn't written his name in a long time. That's the best autograph I've ever received.

That Christmas, I basically said goodbye to my grandfather. I told him I was going overseas to see what trouble I could find.

He said, "All right, you keep yourself safe. I can't wait to see you when you get back."

> *"I only regret that I have but one life to give for my country."*
> —Capt. Nathan Hale

I gave him a big hug and a kiss on the cheek and said, "You've got it, Gramps."

When my cousin went to say goodbye at Christmas, Gramps said, "Okay, Jason, you make sure that you tell Ryan to get me one of those cool Navy SEAL watches."

When my cousin came up to me, he said, "Hey, Gramps just said don't forget to get him a cool Navy SEAL watch."

We laughed at that, but I couldn't remember talking about some cool watches because we wear different types of watches that cost maybe $150. They are great watches, but he made it sound like they were some high-tech watches nobody has ever seen.

That day, sitting in the funeral home with Gramps in his casket, I remembered his request. I took my watch off. It wasn't anything special, but I'd worn it in combat. I put it on his wrist and slid it just underneath his suit cuff. It put a smile on my face. And I said, "You got it, Gramps. You got your cool Navy SEAL watch."

Then tears kicked in hard.

I put my pin in his lapel pocket to protect him in his travels. We had just lost one amazing American soldier. It was difficult for me, but knowing that I sent him off in the right way and that I got the first chance to give him my goodbye meant a lot to me.

At the memorial service, I told the guard that I'd like to present the flag to my aunt. He pulled me aside and said, "We understand that you are a Navy SEAL and you deal with unbelievable things, but brother, this is a very difficult thing to do for your family. It has nothing to do with how tough you are. It's so powerful because you just lost a very precious man in your life."

I took his word for it. They let me march in step with them. We did the call, the gun salute, and I was next to the highest ranking member of the guard. I stood with pride knowing that my grandfather was being honored for a lifetime of service. He never got to see me in uniform, but there I was at his memorial service.

As the guard gave the salute to my aunt holding the American flag, I had to do everything in my power to keep strong. It was so powerful. The guard had been right, I couldn't have made it through the ceremony without breaking down; instead, I was able to stand in respect for him and support her.

I wasn't able to be there for the burial because I had to get back to war before the next mission. My team had granted me access to pay honor to this soldier, watch him go to God, and now it was time to get back to service.

I had dinner that evening with my family and walked around town with my mother the next morning. During the walk we saw this store with a bunch of masks in the window. One of them was of Gene Simmons of KISS.

I had an epiphany. I told my mom, "I've got to go in there real quick."

We went in and I bought face paint for KISS masks. I

wanted to do something memorable in honor of my grand-father. My grandpa knew I like KISS (Detroit, Rock City). I thought having my team paint our faces as KISS when we went out on a mission would be pretty memorable if it didn't get me kicked out of the service.

Twenty-four hours later, I was back in Iraq. There's nothing worse than being away from your platoon, especially when they're in a combat zone. I told three of the guys to dress up and paint our faces like KISS.

We took pictures because we had nothing going on that night. My grandfather would have cracked up seeing us like that. He had a great sense of humor for military things. I'm sure he's proud that we did it in memory of him.

The final piece of the story is when we got back to America, I took three pictures and sent them off to Gene Simmons to show him that KISS had invaded Iraq.

In about three weeks, I got those pictures back from Gene Simmons, autographed, saying, "You guys make us proud. You are true Americans and I'm humbled by you." I know Gene Simmons is a super military supporter, and it's nice to know that people like him support us.

Times change, war has changed, but the traditions of the American soldier remain. The men in World War II created the footprints for the rest of us to follow in. We fight hard today because they fought before us. They are inspirational. Their example motivates us to be that much better as Americans.

CHAPTER 11

SERVICE AFTER SERVICE

In 2009, I started to see a shift in the war in Iraq. Things were dying down and it looked like work would be shifted to Afghanistan. That's when I started thinking that there might be other opportunities. I'd been on three back-to-back deployments and was thinking about other opportunities like instructor duty.

When I got back from deployment around October, I went into instructor duty at Advanced Training Command as a liaison to an intelligence course. That lasted until September of 2010. I knew that if I stayed in another cycle, I would be there for a career; plus, budgets were being cut and troops were being reduced. If we weren't going to be fighting in a war, what would I be doing?

It's hard for a soldier to say, "I served in the military, but I didn't do it during wartime." And that wasn't for me. I wanted to fight in a war or I wanted to do other things. So I decided to leave the military.

My vision for my life outside the military was to go into business, to learn how to do other things besides fighting the war, and to establish myself. A very close friend of mine named Vic Lattimore asked me to come to Dallas to get tied into some key leaders and establish my business career.

"In the final measure, nothing speaks like deeds."
—General John A. Wickham

I took him up on the offer and started my journey.

First, I worked at a company doing personal security. It was a real blessing to decompress from war and jump into a role that somewhat simulates some of our SEAL missions. We took care of private individuals, ensuring their safety and security and that of their families. The job involved traveling, protecting, and thinking tactically about security, safety, and awareness while teaching courses on shooting. I was prepped and ready for the job, and it helped me get into the civilian market.

The owner's dream was to hire veterans to do jobs that would use the skills they learned in the military and in combat. That way, they didn't have to shut down what they'd spent so much time and energy learning.

The boss was generous and introduced me to all his contacts and helped me build his company. For instance, we met with Sam Brown, a former Army Ranger officer. Sam graduated from West Point before becoming a Ranger and being deployed to Afghanistan.

One day his vehicle hit a roadside bomb and he was immediately engulfed in flames. Here was a hero whose life was devastated by his injuries. He lost a close friend that day, but he also took the majority of the blast on his own body. He was burned over 30 percent of his body: his face, hands, arms, back. Skin grafts took skin from other places on his body, so his whole body is scarred.

I had seen injuries overseas, horrific stuff, but seeing Sam in a corporate setting, miles away from war, gave me the realization of just how difficult life can be for these brave soldiers years after they've served.

Sam told me about being in the airport one time, and a little girl looked over at him and said, "Hey, look; it's Freddy Krueger." Kids are brutally honest and transparent, but to a guy like Sam, as tough as he might be, that hurts.

Referring to his burns, I asked, "What are they doing for you guys today?" I know there are all kinds of things that they can do with missing limbs, but I didn't know what they did for burn survivors.

He said, "The doctors did their best on me." He told me he had had 30 surgeries at that point and expected to have many, many more.

I know about the internal demons suffered by every soldier who's been in combat, but I can't imagine what Sam goes through. He said, "I'm here to lead and show you that no matter what happens, you can still get the job done and do it effectively and carry on."

I went home that evening and started doing research about what Sam was facing. But there wasn't much information out there. I searched all night long in my computer room. There wasn't anything.

If you search for "prosthetic companies," you get all sorts of companies that are doing incredible things. But with burns, there is no pipeline. There are hospitals that keep soldiers who are burned through the duration of their major surgeries, but there is no pipeline for civilians or firemen from the point of the burn to acclimating back into society.

I got really pissed off. We've got a guy who fought for our country and he ended up soaking up a bomb. Now there was little support for him and almost no information available to help him.

In the morning, I called Sam and said, "Hey, man; I don't know if you remember me from yesterday."

He said, "Yes; how are you doing?"

I said, "I've been looking online all night for things about burns. I didn't find much. But what I do see is a lot of gaps that need to be filled. If you will allow me, I'd like to take on a mission to construct a program to fill these gaps and create a pipeline for burn survivors. If I do this, would you be in?"

"I would be honored," he said.

I said, "Okay, that's all I needed to hear."

> "Out of every one hundred men, ten shouldn't even be there, eighty are just targets, nine are the real fighters, and we are lucky to have them, for they make the battle. Ah, but the one, one is a warrior, and he will bring the others back."
> —Heraclitus

I went to the drawing board. I remembered a poem by newspaperman George Morrow Mayo, written during World War I referencing the Civil War. In the end, the soldiers from both armies come together as Sons of the Flag. I decided to name my new organization after that line in the poem. It is known as "A Toast" or "Sons of the Flag."

Here's to the Blue of the wind-swept North,
When we meet on the fields of France;

May the spirit of Grant be with you all
As the sons of the North advance!

And here's to the Gray of the sun-kissed South,
When we meet on the fields of France;

May the spirit of Lee be with you all
As the sons of the South advance!

And here's to the Blue and the Gray as one,
When we meet on the fields of France;

May the spirit of God be with you all
As the sons of the Flag advance!

At that point, all I had was a name. I didn't know what to do or where to go. I'd never done this stuff before; in fact, I used to laugh at nonprofits. To a soldier, nonprofits seemed like easy work. You just go out and help people, right?

What I did know is that I needed a team. I reached out to close friends, key business leaders, firemen, and people from the military. I invited them to a meeting at one of my advisor's houses. I said, "I don't know how any of this works, but I'm going to go after it. I need your help."

When we met, we officially created the Sons of the Flag Organization for Burn Survivors.

Our goal at the time was to be a veterans' charity, to help burn survivors with technology and rehabilitation. But as the foundation grew, we discovered that the gaps weren't just for the military; firemen and civilians face similar barriers and gaps. A burn is a burn. It isn't just the soldiers facing a painful future. So we asked ourselves, "Why not cover all?"

Once we became an organization, we took a trip to Brooke Army Medical Center. We met with their top doctors. We learned what they were doing at the hospital, how they treat burned soldiers, and what the future holds for burn survivors. They shared with us new technology and research that was coming. I discovered that there is a lot of stuff that burn survivors are not aware of.

Then two doctors from Brigham and Women's Hospital in Boston came to Dallas to meet with us. They shared with us even more research that was going on and technology that was in development.

There are a lot of burn units in the country; some are very large and some small, but not all of them do primary research and development. The surgeries are very complex. The skin always mutates, and they have to play a waiting game with burn survivors until they see what their skin decides to do.

As a new foundation, we are tied in with doctors because we feel we have a lot of learning to do. The doctors see the technology and work with it.

That being said, the burn survivors are the ones who go through the surgeries. They wake up feeling tight, or having an abscess on their skin, or maybe a wound is getting infected. So while we can learn a lot from the doctors, the burn survivors are the key ingredient to learning where the gaps are in the burn community.

Unlike a wound where you get a prosthetic that can be worn under your clothes, burn survivors typically have wounds on their faces and hands. A lot of survivors are nervous to wear their skin proudly, and they don't like the reactions they get from the public.

> "Nothing is as strong as the heart of a volunteer."
>
> —LTC Jimmy Doolittle, WWII

For instance, one day I was at a local diner when a burn survivor walked in. I didn't know what to say to him, so I said nothing. I thought, "What a bunch of bullshit. I'm a coward. I'm trying to run an organization for burn survivors, and I just let him walk by?"

I was really down on myself and determined that from then on, I would know what to say to empower burn survivors. I would talk with them about their injuries and learn from them.

It wasn't three months later that I was eating at a different place, and the same man came in. I walked up to him with my business card and asked, "How did you earn your wounds?"

He shared his story with me, and I told him a little about Sons of the Flag.

I received a note from him later about how impressed

he was with what we are doing. He wanted to sit down with us and talk about the gaps not being filled. He also wanted to join our team.

Now I know how to approach people. I ask them, "How did you earn your wounds?" I talk with them about their injuries and the gaps that need to be filled. As an organization, we are not solely about research and technology. We want to make sure survivors get the care they need. We want to limit infection and help with pain management. We also look into the future. When we see new technology and treatments, we get excited.

Like any team with a mission, there are still hiccups and problems, but we are learning where to put our money to actually benefit burn survivors. Sons of the Flag has gone from being a research-based community to a network. It is now a portal for people who have gone through the initial hospitalization, but are unsure what comes next. We have them covered: mind, body, and financially. We are showing burn survivors and families what to expect, where to go, who to talk to, and we help if there are financial needs. The more people who know about us, the easier it will be to develop a database with a support system.

When people get burned, they may be in the hospital from six months to a year or more. The family may have to move from where they live to be closer to the patient. Then there is follow-up care outside the hospital. Dressings and bandages have to be changed and appointments for treatment met. Many survivors can't drive because of damage to their hands.

As an organization, it's about looking at what needs to be corrected and making it happen. Every day, we are blessed to talk with burn survivors who are willing to share their stories, even though it pains them to talk about it.

I'm absolutely blessed to run Sons of the Flag, but it also pisses me off that we are here. Sons of the Flag should not be needed. There should have already been something out there for those who are injured. There should be better processes in place.

Sons of the Flag has helped me to cope with getting out of the service. I call it "service after service" because soldiers want to continue to serve even when they are no longer in the military. Some men will do 20 to 30 years in the military; others will get out relatively early, like me. But like me, they all want to continue their service. It is part of our make-up, our DNA.

I feel like I'm serving my country as much now as when I was fighting bad guys overseas. Why? Because Sons of the Flag dramatically impacts people inside the USA.

I've met an incredible number of people along the way. Every burn survivor has a different story. They have different stories about how they got through it and how they continue to fight through it. In my opinion, burns are one of the worst injuries you can have. And burn survivors are some of the toughest people I know.

CHAPTER 12

THE LEGACY JUMP
11/17/12

The first thing I did on "Jump" day, November 17, 2012, was go outside to check the weather. All the efforts we had put into creating the Legacy Jump, the work to get the veterans lined up, the pilots and jump team organized, giving the volunteers their duties, even figuring out how workers were going to get fed, all of that depended upon a clear day. Low clouds or storms could sideline the whole thing.

So you can imagine how on edge I was that morning, not to mention emotional about how much was riding on me and the weather. We were about to do something that had never been done before. Our mission was clear. And every obstacle could be overcome except for the weather.

I almost cried when I saw a clear day. We were a go.

There aren't enough pages in this book to even outline all the organization and work that went into launching the Legacy Jump. Fortunately, I had a great team supporting me.

As soon as I saw it was going to be clear day, I got to work preparing for the men coming in from out of town. We had some guys who hadn't jumped before and others who hadn't jumped in 50 years.

John Walters was the first to show up at my house. I could feel his nervousness in the face of his first jump. I joked that he'd better make sure his artificial leg was strapped on well or it would become a missile falling out of the sky.

A friend of mine picked up Peter Bielskis at the airport and brought him over to my house. He had gotten up early for the flight from Detroit. I knew he had to be tired, but again, his nervousness had him alert. He was also facing his first jump at the age of 88.

All morning long, I kept looking up at the sky, checking to see if it was clear. Banking on good weather in Texas in November for a skydive is like betting on green at the roulette table.

We showed up at the airport early. The first thing I did was talk to Doug Jeans, the executive director of Cavanaugh Flight Museum. He had the planes fueled and ready to go. He even had our logo on the side of the DC3 we'd be using for the jump.

I checked to make sure our gear was laid out and good to go. Nobody had seen the jumpsuits because I wanted it to be a surprise. The men asked what they needed to wear, and I told them we had them covered.

Soon, people started showing up. The look on each of their faces was "Holy cow; I can't believe this is really happening."

As for me? I started to feel overwhelmed. It was all on me. It would be the most amazing event ever or a complete failure depending on how well we performed. This was my first major event like this, and I wanted everything crisp and absolutely perfect.

> *"I'd rather go down the river with seven studs than with a hundred shitheads."*
> —Colonel Charlie Beckwith, founder & CMDR of Delta Force

Fortunately, my comrade Russ Spears was there to take over the show. He ended up being the man in control, the operations guy. And he did a kick-ass job. I could not have completed that jump without him.

All the jumpers were there except Salvatore. When I asked him to represent Afghanistan in the jump, he said, "Oh, man, I'm in. Just let me know the date." The problem with the date was that he had a golf ceremony the morning of the jump. So when he did show up, he was in dress slacks and a dress shirt. He jumped straight into his jumpsuit like he was James Bond, and he was ready to go.

Tom Buning also had a conflict. He was actually in Florida that weekend. As the associate athletic director at SMU in Texas, one of his teams was playing in the finals during that weekend. While his team was good, he couldn't have predicted they'd be in the finals the day of the jump. So he flew back to Dallas on Friday night to jump on Saturday and then flew back to Florida to be with his team. Talk about commitment.

Besides the jump, we had other things for people to see. There were vintage airplanes from the museum lined up. We had tanks and all sorts of fire rigs, from old to new.

When the jump team arrived, I reviewed logistics with them. Then we gathered the team to give them a jump brief along with a mini-class on how things would go once we were in the plane. Finally, everyone had to sign waivers.

Of course, that's when some complications arrived and I had to leave the group to get things settled.

Finally we were ready. Russ got everyone to the drop zone. We went through the final checks and procedures. Then it was time to load up.

My dad called right then to tell me there were over 500 people on the airfield to watch us jump. This was a private drop zone, and yet all these people were there to witness history.

Stepping into the World War II-era plane was almost overwhelming. Five years of dreaming, planning, and work were coming to this point.

We had a man from every war from World War II to the present, shoulder to shoulder, dedicated to the same mission. There's nothing like being in the presence of the entire legacy who are still living and to be the soldier in the newer era looking at men who paved the way for me.

I remember laughing because I'm a skydiver. At that point, I had already done a few jumps. And now I was going to jump in tandem, something I hadn't done since I was 17. I don't know if it was the event itself, all that I had riding on the jump, or jumping in a way I haven't in a long time, but even I was nervous.

Since I needed to be on the ground looking over things, I was up first to jump. The leader of the jump team, Greg, stood with me, clicking me into the harness, connecting us.

Jumping out of a plane is a lot different than people think. When you go tandem, you are suspended out of the plane when you are 15,000 feet in the air. You are just dangling there, tied to your tandem partner. He's got all the weight as you hang, waiting to launch.

For a non-jumper, this can be an overwhelming feeling because you don't know what to expect.

You get a three-two-one launch. You lean backward. And when your tandem partner launches from the plane, you essentially do a barrel roll.

Once you're out of the plane, it's a whole different ball game. It's a playground up there. You don't have that sinking feeling in the pit of your stomach like you do on a rollercoaster because you are already moving at terminal velocity. The only way you know you're falling is because of the wind on your face and the noise in your ears. But it doesn't feel like you are soaring over 100 miles an hour toward the earth. It is such a large landscape and you have such a view, you can't tell how fast you are moving.

When you are in tandem, it is the tandem coach who controls things. All you do is keep your arms spread apart and your feet behind you, and he takes control of the ride. He is going to turn you a couple of times to the right or left, and you are going to see the entire world before you.

It's such a groovy feeling.

Then the tandem coach will tap your hand or give you a thumbs-up to let you know he is getting ready to pull the chute. When that happens, you go from moving very fast downward to a floating stop, hopefully.

This is the part you don't understand from watching

videos. The camera guy is moving so quickly toward the earth that when you pull your chute, it looks like you're yanked upward. In reality, it's a calm, peaceful feeling. It's an illusion of the camera moving with you, then speeding away from you.

Once you're under canopy, it's quiet and relaxing. You can see birds flying by you. Your tandem coach will move you toward the drop zone and turn you a few times to see the whole landscape. You feel the cool breezes on your face. It's just you up there with nothing else to focus on. No work-related issues or problems bothering you. You are in the sky and soaring.

That is, until the last few seconds. Your tandem coach pulls you into position for the landing. Then, right before you hit the ground, you get into your half-break position, ready to land. But just before you hit the ground, the tandem coach slows your fall all the way down. Sometimes you may even land standing up. You might be staggering a bit with the change from soaring through the sky to having landed on your feet, but there really is no stress involved.

Once you're on the ground, you look up and see the plane all the way up there. You realize that's how far you've come in a few short minutes. You left the plane at 15,000 feet above the birds, and now you're here on the ground. It's an incredible maneuver.

As we came into the landing zone that day, the speakers were playing Lee Greenwood singing, "Proud to Be an American." Everyone on the ground was screaming and cheering. I was very emotional by the time I hit the ground. This is really happening; people are here to support the legacy of the troops. It was surreal.

We hit the ground, and my mom was the first one to

run up to me and give me a big hug. Then my buddy Pryor, who I thought wasn't going to make it, hugged me. He's one of my closest brothers. Then it was a blur of hugs and handshakes as the plane circled overhead, preparing to release the next guys.

This second pass was the new guys. Salvatore from Afghanistan, then T.Y. from Iraq, then John Walters from the New York Fire Department, and finally Tom from Desert Storm. It was cool to see these amazingly iconic men floating down to us.

The plane landed so we could load up the old guys. We moved them to the loading area in an old Huey helicopter. It was a great pre-

> *"We must learn to live together as brothers or perish together as fools."*
> —Martin Luther King, Jr.

sentation of these men to the crowd as they boarded the plane and prepared for the jump.

Russ Spears went up with the old guys. He had worked so hard putting this event together, making sure everything that I had planned was complete. He put his heart and soul into it. But Russ had never jumped before. I said, "I've got a jumpsuit for you. You're the captain of the team; what do you think?"

I could see nervousness going on. But he still strapped on the jumpsuit and got his gear locked in. I knew he was about to experience the coolest thing of his lifetime.

Russ jumped out after the old guys. Imagine seeing a legacy of soldiers exiting a plane before your own eyes. It's extremely inspirational.

While the old guys were preparing to jump, I stood by ground control so I could hear how things were going. The first jumper popped out—Tony representing Vietnam.

Then Dick popped out representing the Korean War.

So much was riding on Peter from World War II. If he didn't make it out, we would not have completed our mission. But it was Peter's first dive and at 88 years old!

While I watched, the bird cruised farther from the drop zone. I was starting to get worried. What if there were complications? What if Peter simply decided not to do it?

I looked at ground control. He pointed at me, then raised two fingers for World War II, and then he gave me a thumbs up.

I looked back to the sky, and sure enough there was a little dot floating away from the plane. I watched until the chute opened up. We'd completed the legacy skydive. We'd nailed it.

An interesting side note: For the second legacy skydive, Peter Bielskis had some issues at home, so we weren't sure if he was going to make it. We had to figure out who we were going to call for World War II. Finding a World War II guy who wants to jump out of a plane is pretty close to impossible—not impossible—but close.

A friend, who is a fireman in Dallas, had a relative who served in the Navy in World War II. His name is Art Black. We called him and asked if he'd like to jump from a perfectly good airplane with soldiers from every other war. He said, "You know...Wow, that's a good question. All right, I'll do it."

We told him when and where it was to be held, and he said, "I'll drive on out from Oklahoma. We'll do this."

Then the day before the skydive, Peter decided everything was cleared up. He called to ask if I still wanted him.

I said, "Yeah, come on with us."

So we ended up breaking the record by having two World War II skydivers that year.

Each one of the divers was ready to get after it, regardless of his nervousness and worries. We were able to look across the generations of war. We were each part of a proud American legacy.

There's something about that vision that will be ingrained in my memory forever. Those men proved that service never ends. You aren't a soldier for four years and then you are done. You have that mentality and character for the rest of your life.

So the question is *why*? Why do we do what we do? The answer is simple: It's for those to the left of us and to the

Left to right: *Art Black, Dick Agnew, John Walters, Peter Bielskis, Tom Buning, T.Y., Tony Bandiera, Sal Giunta*

right of us. It's because America's worth it. We are all Sons of the Flag.

God bless everyone in harm's way, whether overseas or in America. Remember that the brotherhood never forgets what each of you does for freedom.

America is strong because of sacrifice. She is secure because her citizens are responsible to and for each other. And she'll have a solid future because of our dedication to the mission.

Acknowledgements

Richard "Dick" Agnew
Omar Avila
Cody B.
Brad Bacon & Family
Faye Bacon
Matt Bacon
Bobby Baker
Tony Bandiera
Tom Barnes
Peter Bielskis
J.P. Blacksmith & Family
Pryor Blackwell
Connie Boucher
Sam & Amy Brown
Clint Bruce
Tom Buning
Ronald Campbell
Dr. E.J. Caterson
Jamie Coates
William Corrigan
Dallas Fire Rescue
Sasha & Jeff Denman
Cdr. Clyde George Gardner, Jr.
Susan Gardner Donovan
Matthew Edwards
Sal Giunta
Vlada Gorbaneva
Bobby Halton
Mark Hayes
Richard Hayner
Hayner Family
Ryan & Carolyn Hyman
Doug Jeans
Shelly Kirkland
Zane Krempin
Chris Kyle Family
Ben L.
Ace Lane
Vic Lattimore

Josh Lewis
Jeff Malczynski
Christopher McIntyre
Mary Denton Meier
Raymond Naamou
Tommy Norris
Naval Special Warfare
Scott O'Grady
Caston Parrott
Parrott Family
Patrick Parrott
Jonathan Peters PhD
Nathan Pilcher
Robert Raymond
Benjamin Reeves
Stephen Schmidt
Reggie Showers
Bill Shufford
Scott Simson
Jerry Smith
Luke Snyder
Russ Spears
Gary Tanner
Willie Thompson
Michael Thornton, CMH
Greg Turnell
United States Air Force
United States Army
United States Marine Corps
United States Navy
John Walters III
Robert Wiedmann
Greg Windmiller
Lisa Wolf
Steve Woods
David Worley
Paul Yount